Prentice Hall

CONSTITUTION STUDY GUIDE

CONSTITUTION STUDY GUIDE

Prentice Hall   Needham, Massachusetts   Upper Saddle River, New Jersey

CONSTITUTION STUDY GUIDE

PRENTICE HALL

A VIACOM COMPANY

Upper Saddle River, New Jersey 07458

© 1996 by Prentice Hall, Needham, Massachusetts and Upper Saddle River, New Jersey

ISBN 0-13-423989-x

3456789-DBH-999897

Table of Contents

The American Constitution is based on the belief that the American people are the source of the government's power.

To appreciate the enormous impact the U.S. Constitution has on your life, imagine for a moment that it had never existed. The United States might have remained the loose confederation of highly independent, squabbling states it was in 1787. Some of these states might even have broken away eventually and declared themselves separate nations.

Suppose that you and your family visited a neighboring state last weekend. Without a constitution, you might have had to produce a passport to enter the state. Or perhaps that state might not have permitted anyone of your race or religious background to visit it.

Now suppose that you wanted to send a letter to your local newspaper strongly criticizing your state's governor. Without a constitution, you might not have the right to express your opinion freely. The newspaper might reject your letter because it only prints articles that the state government writes and approves. The governor might order you to be arrested and kept in jail for years without a trial.

Finally, suppose that you were alive during World War II. Without a constitution the separate states might not have had the ability to organize a common defense. Some may even have been at war with each other already. In the midst of this confusion and weakness, a foreign nation might have invaded and conquered the North American continent.

It is easy to overlook the impact of the Constitution on our daily lives. Because we have lived under it so long, we take it for granted, in the same way that we take breathing for granted. But just as we need oxygen to live, we need the Constitution to organize our system of government and protect our basic freedoms.

The Constitution affects much of what we do. It provides for the laws that control the food we eat, the products that we buy, and the schools we attend. It protects our freedom to express our opinions and criticize our leaders. It defends our choice of religion and guarantees us equal opportunity under the law, whatever our race, sex, or national background. Most important of all, it allows us to live our lives largely the way we choose.

Written more than 200 years ago, the U.S. Constitution was the first attempt in history to design a national government on paper. After 200 years and only a few changes, it is still the legal document that defines our system of government. The Constitution has enjoyed this long history of success for three main reasons. First, its authors understood the vision Americans had for their new nation. Second, the Framers created a flexible document, one that could be adapted as society changed. And third, the Constitution affects the daily lives of every citizen of the United States, whether they be adults or young people.

How much do you know about the Constitution and the impact it has on your life? The following questions allow you to test your knowledge. Subsequent sections review the constitutional issues that young Americans face and illustrate the way the Constitution has influenced other governments and groups.

"If a nation expects to be ignorant and free, in a state of civilization, it expects what never was and never will be."

– Thomas Jefferson

How much do you know about the Constitution?

The following questions test your knowledge of how the U.S. Constitution affects the lives of young people. Answer each question true or false. There is a total of 10 points.

1. All Americans have an unlimited right to freedom of expression.

2. The U.S. Constitution recognizes that the good of society must outweigh the rights of the individual.

3. A young person can be asked to testify against himself or herself in a juvenile court proceeding.

4. A juvenile has a right to a lawyer if accused of a crime.

5. Minors have the same right to trial by jury as an adult.

6. High school students have the right to conduct a political demonstration at school.

7. A principal or superintendent can stop the publication of a school newspaper if it is saying bad things about the school.

8. If a juvenile is arrested, his or her parents must be informed immediately.

9. If a school official searches your locker without a search warrant, nothing that is found can be used against you.

10. Young people have the same rights under the U.S. Constitution as adults.

When you finish the unit on the Constitution, take this quiz again. Your teacher will give you the correct answers to the quiz questions at that time. Give yourself one point for each correct answer. Then compare your two performances on the quiz and rate yourself on the scale below.

9 or 10 right — Constitutional Scholar
7 or 8 right — Knowledgeable Citizen
5 or 6 right — Average Person on the Street
4 or fewer right — You are not looking out for your own rights!

Constitutional Issues Confront the Lives of Students

Young Americans face constitutional issues that their parents and grandparents never confronted. Views about the rights of minors have changed. Young people today enjoy many of the constitutional rights and protections of adults. Several activities in this study guide examine the constitutional rights of young people.

Young people who come into contact with juvenile authorities have many of the protections of adults. They have a right to have a lawyer represent them. They have the right to equal protection of the law.

Eighteen-year-olds gained the right to vote in federal elections in 1971 with the ratification of the Twenty-sixth Amendment. Many states granted voting rights in state and local elections to eighteen-year-olds at about the same time.

Children are gaining a say for themselves in cases involving the family. In divorce cases in many states, the feelings of children in the family are considered when custody is granted. The courts watch cases of corporal punishment closely to ensure that children are not injured as a result of punishment. Child abuse, which in the past was viewed as a family matter, is now treated as a crime. Not all these matters reflect constitutional questions. However, they demonstrate the growing rights that young people have gained.

Juveniles do not have all the constitutional rights of adults. For example, only adults are guaranteed a jury trial. Juvenile justice systems are designed to treat children differently. Juveniles are not considered criminals. Since they have not reached the age of adulthood, the courts feel that juveniles should not be held fully responsible for their actions.

Views are changing about the place of young people in American life. As a result, young people face many adult constitutional issues. Young people and adults alike are concerned about such issues as registration for Selective Service, the rights of teenage mothers, school prayer, and student clubs that discriminate, among other issues. There is hardly a junior or senior high school in the country that has not faced some of these issues. Like adults, young people are divided over such issues. Their concerns guarantee that the Supreme Court will continue to evaluate the rights and protections granted to juveniles under the Constitution.

Student government is modeled on the federal system

Other governments and organizations follow the model of the U.S. Constitution in their own constitutions or rules. State constitutions commonly parallel the federal document. Many student councils also use the U.S. Constitution as their model.

The student council constitution of Shaler Area Intermediate High School is a good example of the Constitution's influence. Shaler Area Intermediate High School is located in suburban Pittsburgh, Pennsylvania. It is composed of the seventh, eighth, and ninth grades.

Like the federal Constitution, the Shaler student council constitution is divided into articles, sections, and clauses. Its first article describes the purpose of the student council constitution, just as the Preamble of the U.S. Constitution describes the purpose of the document. The lists at right compare other similarities between the Shaler student council constitution and the U.S. Constitution.

U.S. Constitution

Article I includes the requirements to be a member of Congress: a Representative must be at least 25 years old and a citizen for 7 years; a Senator must be at least 30 years old and a citizen for 9 years; and all must be inhabitants of the state from which they are elected.

Article I grants the power of election of the leaders of the houses of Congress. The House membership elects its Speaker. The Senate is led by the Vice President, and the Senators elect a President Pro Tempore who serves in the Vice President's absence.

Section 5 of Article I sets out the rules of Congress. For example, the House and Senate make the rules for conducting their business. Each house of Congress must keep a daily record of its activities. When in session, neither house can adjourn for more than 3 days unless both houses agree.

Under Article I, Section 7, the president has the power to veto legislation.

Article VII provides for ratification of the Constitution. Nine states had to approve the Constitution by a vote of special conventions.

Either house of Congress can propose amendments to the Constitution, under the provisions of Article V. A two-thirds vote of both houses is required to pass amendments. Three-fourths of the states must approve an amendment to ratify it.

Shaler Student Council Constitution

Article II describes the requirements of membership in the Shaler Area Intermediate High School Student Council: Each representative must maintain a "C" average and be a member of the group or social studies class which elects him or her.

Article III describes the duties and responsibilities of the Chairperson, Recording Secretary, Representatives, and Advisor.

Article IV sets the rules of procedure for the Student Council. Each representative gets one vote. A simple majority decides issues that do not involve spending money. Money issues require a two-thirds vote. Meetings follow Robert's Rules of Order. Three unexcused absenses result in dismissal from Student Council.

Under Article IV, Section 5, the principal and activities director maintain the power of veto over the decisions of the student council.

Under Article VI, the student council constitution is ratified by a two-thirds vote of the student body.

A two-thirds vote of the student council will pass an amendment under Article VI. Ratification requires a two-thirds vote of the student body.

How does your school compare?

Does your school have a student council or forum? Read its constitution and compare it to the U.S. Constitution, as in the example from Shaler Area Intermediate High School above.

Other Case Studies

Each of the following four chapters in this study guide contains a case study describing a Supreme Court case. Each of these studies examines the rights of young people under the U.S. Constitution. In some rulings the Court's justices extended those rights to young people.

Each case study describes the incident that eventually resulted in an appeal to the U.S. Supreme Court. It presents the arguments for and against the young people involved.

You will decide how you think the Supreme Court should have ruled in each case. Then you will write a court "opinion" describing why you think the case should be decided that way.

1 The Roots of Constitutional Government

In September, 1987, Americans gathered outside Independence Hall in Philadelphia to celebrate the bicentennial of the U.S. Constitution.

Chapter Outline

About This Chapter

On September 17, 1987, thousands of people from across the nation gathered outside Independence Hall in Philadelphia. They were there to celebrate the writing, some 200 years before, of the U.S. Constitution.

There, over a period of four months, the Framers of the Constitution debated, wrote, and revised their nation's future. They labored during the hottest summer months in a building with sealed windows and without air conditioning. Outside, hay and gravel were strewn on the cobblestones so that the clatter of passing carriages would not disturb their discussions.

The Framers were all white males who wore powdered wigs and wool suits. But 200 years later, the plan of government they produced would have to serve women, blacks, Hispanics, American Indians, Asians, and other immigrant groups, as well as those wearing jeans and gym shoes.

The ideas and events that shaped the thinking of the Constitution's writers developed over many years. Abuses the colonists faced from the English government influenced the Framers' thinking. So too, did the ideas on government developed in Europe in the 1700s and 1800s. Other factors that influenced the people who wrote the Constitution were the successes and failures of their early experiment with self-government during and after the Revolution. These influences are the subject of this chapter.

1 Americans Declare Their Independence

As you read, think about answers to these questions:
★ Why did the colonists rebel against Britain?
★ How did the colonists establish their independence?
★ What are the basic human rights demanded in the Declaration of Independence?

From the time of first settlement in the early 1600s until 1776, the American colonies were under British control. The king of England appointed governors who ruled the colonists. These governors had the power to carry out the king's wishes and enforce British laws. In reality, however, colonial governors often allowed the colonists quite a bit of freedom. This policy, known as *salutary,* or beneficial, *neglect* was in place for many decades.

For most of the colonial period, locally elected assemblies decided how to deal with the day-to-day issues that affected the colonists. Members of the colonial assemblies passed their own acts, including tax laws. The king and his royal governors did not mind letting the colonists rule themselves as long as the colonies supplied Britain with materials for British industries and bought British-made goods. Until the mid-1700s, this system satisfied the needs of both Britain and the American colonies. In the mid-1700s, however, relations between the king of England and the American colonists grew tense.

salutary neglect British policy that allowed American colonists to rule themselves so long as Britain also benefitted

★ The Colonists Rebel

After fighting and winning a seven-year long war against France, Britain was left with a huge war debt. Because Britain had fought to protect the colonies, the king and *Parliament* decided in 1763 that the colonies should pay taxes to relieve the war debt. In addition, Britain began to enforce laws that required all goods shipped to and from the colonies to be carried on British ships. Because British ships used British ports, Britain could tax the goods going to or coming from the colonies. This was another way Britain hoped to raise more money to pay its bills. In general, Britain wanted more control over the colonies. The colonists, on the other hand, were used to governing themselves and resented the interference. Eventually this conflict developed into the American Revolution. Historians have noted three kinds of problems — economic, social, and political — that caused the rebellion in 1776.

Parliament British law-making body

Social Problems. The great distance between the colonies and Britain led many colonists to think of themselves as Americans rather than as English citizens. The colonists grew used to solving their own problems. When local authorities acting in behalf of the king or Parliament attempted to enforce laws telling the colonists how to do things, the colonists became resentful.

Economic Problems. Many of the laws that Parliament made concerned economic ties between Britain and the colonies. Britain wanted access to the colonies' raw materials. British companies used these resources to manufacture goods. Britain also wanted the colonists to buy only goods made in Britain. For example, owners of the British iron industry wanted to buy American iron ore at a discounted price. In addition, they wanted the colonists to buy British iron products rather than those manufactured in the colonies. Many colonists, however, felt that such British trade and manufacturing policies favored Britain and hurt the colonies. This led to more tension between Americans and the British.

Political Problems. By the 1760s, these social and economic tensions had developed into a serious political dispute. Between 1765 and 1770, Parliament twice placed new taxes on the colonies. Both times the colonists protested and Britain *repealed* the taxes. Why did the colonists oppose British taxes? Many Americans openly objected to these taxes because they believed in the principle of no taxation without *representation*. Because the colonists were not represented in Parliament, they felt it unfair to be subject to British tax laws. Secretly, however, many colonists were becoming less concerned about the issue of representation in Britain's Parliament. They felt they were better qualified to tax themselves — and even to rule themselves. The colonists wanted independence!

As the colonists anger increased, many began to think the time had come to throw off British rule and declare American independence. During 1775 and 1776, many colonists talked and thought about setting up an independent nation. The writings of certain leaders helped bring about this more *revolutionary* approach.

In January 1776, Thomas Paine published a pamphlet called *Common Sense*. Paine argued that the colonists should declare their independence from Britain because King George III showed no willingness to grant tax reforms or greater self-rule. Paine asked anyone "to show a single advantage this continent can reap by being connected with Britain . . ." and added, "since nothing but blows will do . . . let us come to a final separation."

★ The Colonists Representatives Call for Independence

Paine's pamphlet and the growing anger of the colonists had an effect on the *Continental Congress*, too. The Continental Congress was a group of delegates whom the colonists elected to represent the 13 colonies. The delegates had met since 1775 to decide how to respond to British policies.

Congress Responds. By 1776, more and more members of Congress had come to believe that the colonies must declare independence. In June 1776, the Second Continental Congress was held. A delegate from Virginia, Richard Henry Lee, offered a resolution saying that "these United Colonies are, and of right ought to be, free and independent States." Congress appointed a committee, headed by another Virginian, Thomas Jefferson, to prepare such a declaration. At the same time, Congress advised the 13 new states to set up their own governments. On July 2, 1776, Jefferson presented his draft of the *Declaration of Independence* to Congress. After making some changes in the document, the Second Continental Congress voted to accept the Declaration on July 4.

repeal officially withdraw

representation elected leadership

revolutionary favoring a great change

Continental Congress elected representatives advising the colonists on policies regarding relations with Britain

8

★ The Declaration of Independence States Americans' Rights and Grievances

The Declaration of Independence contains both a statement of basic human rights and government responsibilities, and a list of grievances against the British Crown.

Stating Their Rights. Thomas Jefferson outlined several basic rights at the beginning of the document:

We hold these truths to be self-evident, that all men are created equal, that they are endowed by their Creator with certain unalienable Rights, that among these are Life, Liberty, and the pursuit of Happiness.

Many colonists believed that there were certain truths, or basic facts, about human beings that all governments should recognize. What are these truths? The first truth is that "all men (all people) are created equal." That is, all people are born with the same rights. The second truth is that government cannot take away certain rights given to people by God or nature. These include "Life, Liberty, and the pursuit of Happiness." Governments are set up by human beings, Jefferson wrote, "to secure these rights." Government, in other words, is the means by which people make sure that every person has these rights. Government gets its power through the people's consent or agreement. The people agree to be governed.

What if government should seek to take away people's natural rights? Then people have both a right and a duty to change the government. As Jefferson wrote, the people have the right "to abolish" a government that disregards their rights.

Jefferson's words showed how many colonists felt. They felt they had good reasons for seeking independence. Britain had, in their view, taken away many of their basic rights.

Listing Their Grievances. Jefferson also presented a list of grievances, showing how the King had abused the colonists. The grievances included "imposing taxes on us without our consent . . . cutting off our trade with all parts of the world . . . and . . . abolishing our most valuable laws." These grievances were constantly kept in mind when the Framers met in Philadelphia to write the Constitution. The Constitution specifically protects Americans against the kinds of abuses suffered by the colonists.

Declaring War. The Declaration of Independence severed political ties with Britain. Having stated that the colonies were now independent states, the colonists were declaring war against Britain. The war lasted from 1776 until 1783.

While the Declaration stated the values of a new nation, it did not provide a plan for creating a government. In 1783, there were no democratic governments anywhere in the world. Thus, Americans did not have an example to follow as they put together a new plan of government. Developing a set of rules governing the country and creating government offices to carry out the rules did not occur overnight. It took years of experimenting before Americans came up with a workable system. In 1787, the Framers met in Philadelphia and wrote the Constitution. Remarkably, this plan of government still guides the United States 200 years later.

Thomas Jefferson, only 33 years old in 1776, completed the Declaration of Independence in two weeks. Jefferson later served as the third President of the United States.

American colonists assembled outside Independence Hall on July 8, 1776, to hear the first reading of the Declaration of Independence.

Section 1 Review

1. **Defining Constitutional Terms**

   Write a brief definition for each of the following terms:

   a. Continental Congress _____

   b. representation _____

   c. Parliament _____

   d. revolutionary _____

   e. repealed _____

   f. salutary neglect _____

2. **Reviewing Social Studies Skills:** Analyzing a Quotation

   Read the quote below. Then examine the statements below which interpret the meaning of the quote. Circle the letter next to the statement that best explains the quote:

   "This new World hath been the asylum for the persecuted lovers of civil and religious liberty from every part of Europe. Hither they have fled, not from the tender embraces of the mother, but from the cruelty of the monster; it is so far true of England that the same tyranny which drove the first emigrants from home, pursues their descendants still."

   —Thomas Paine in *Common Sense*—

   a. All European nations deny their citizens rights to civil and religious freedom.

   b. American colonists fled Europe to get away from their mothers.

   c. American colonists suffered because their basic civil and religious freedoms were denied by the English government.

   d. Britain always protected the rights of American colonists.

3. **Reviewing the Main Ideas**

   Write a brief answer — one or two sentences — for each of the following questions:

   a. Give two reasons why the colonists rebelled against Britain. _____

   _____

   _____

   b. What two steps did Congress take to establish American independence? _____

   _____

   _____

   c. What are two basic human rights stated in the Declaration of Independence? _____

   _____

   _____

4. **Critical Thinking Skills:** Understanding the Constitution

   Once the Continental Congress signed the Declaration of Independence, Americans considered the thirteen colonies to be free and independent states. Still, the states had to fight against Britain to become a truly independent nation. On a separate piece of paper, write a paragraph discussing the kinds of problems the new nation had to solve.

2 European Influences

As you read, think about answers to these questions.

★ What important ideas did the Ancient Greeks and Romans contribute to the American system of government?

★ What contributions did the English make to the development of American government?

★ How did European political philosphers influence the Framers of the U.S. Constitution?

Human beings have been living together in groups for thousands of years. For as long as people have lived in groups, they have felt the need for some type of organization that provides order. Without order, a society would be in chaos, the few constantly trying to assert their will over the many. A government is a way to create order in a society. For example, in your school, the teachers and the principal are, in effect, the government. And students are the governed. You may not always agree with school policies and rules, but imagine what school would be like if there were no rules! After they declared independence from Britain in 1776, Americans needed to form a government. Where did the ideas that Americans put into practice come from? There were three main sources of the ideas that shaped the American plan of government: (1) Ancient Greece and Rome, (2) English history, and (3) European philosophers.

★ Ancient Greeks and Romans Contributed Ideas on Government

The first societies to experiment with ideas on government that would later influence Americans were Ancient Greece and Rome. The Ancient Greeks and Romans developed the ideas of democracy and representative government more than 2,000 years ago.

A Democracy in Ancient Greece. The cities of Ancient Greece were organized into city-states, or small independent nations. Athens was one such city-state. For many years, Athens was ruled by a small group of wealthy and powerful men known as the Great Council. Members of the Council passed laws that favored wealthy people like themselves. Between 750 B.C. and 550 B.C., however, this system of rule began to change.

Poorer Athenians, such as farmers and small merchants, protested the great power of the Council. They believed that the laws made by the Council harmed the interests of the middle-class and poor. Many Greeks wanted to participate directly in making laws affecting their lives. Greeks used the word *demos kratia*, to explain what they wanted. The equivalent word in English is *democracy*, which means government by the people.

Gradually, Athenian leaders agreed that more Greeks should be allowed to participate in the Great Council's decision-making process. They developed a political system now known as a *direct democracy*. In a direct democracy, people not only vote for leaders, but actually serve in the government.

"If liberty and equality, as is thought by some, are chiefly to be found in democracy, they will be best attained when all persons alike share in the government to the utmost."
— *Aristotle*

democracy *government by the people*
direct democracy *a system of government in which people participate directly in decision making through voting on issues*

citizenship *the status of a citizen, or member of a country, with all its duties, rights, and privileges*

In order to decide who should be allowed to serve in the Great Council, Greek leaders developed the idea of *citizenship*. Those Athenians who were citizens had the right to participate directly in government. But how was citizenship determined? Greek leaders decided that only men who owned large plots of land were citizens. Women, slaves, and people with little or no property were not given the rights and responsibilities of Athenian citizenship. While the Ancient Greeks restricted democratic rights to a small portion of the population, the idea of democracy was born.

republic *a system of government in which people elect representatives to govern them; also known as representative government*

A Republic in Ancient Rome. Ancient Rome was the first nation to create a *republic*. A republic is a form of government in which people elect representatives to govern them. Between 750 B.C. and 350 B.C., the Romans established a republic. At first, only patricians — members of the Roman upper-class — were allowed to vote or serve as representatives. Over several centuries, however, the right to vote was extended to plebians — the lower class. As more Romans gained the right to vote, they used their new power to bring about other changes in the political system.

About 450 B.C. Roman citizens demanded that laws governing their lives be written down. They wanted to know what the laws were and that laws could not be changed any time their leaders wanted to. Many Romans believed that codified, or written, laws would prevent Roman leaders from abusing their power.

Ancient Greek and Roman ideas and practices concerning government eventually spread to Europe and to the United States.

★ English History influenced American Thinking on Government

absolute monarch *an all-powerful king and queen*

The first European nation to experiment with democracy was Britain. For many centuries, Britain was ruled by an *absolute monarch*. The king and queen were very powerful rulers. They had the power to do almost anything they wanted. Between 1100 and 1200, however, the English political system began to change.

English common law. In the 1100s, King Henry II attempted to expand the power of the monarchy. One way he did this was by strengthening the royal court system. The king established courts throughout the country. The king's judges assembled juries to hear cases involving crimes and disputes. The king's judges made the laws that these juries used to resolve disputes and to decide whether a person was guilty of a crime. Royal judges made laws based on the customs of the people. The royal courts decisions were gradually written down and became the basis for *common law*. Under common law, the courts applied the same legal ideas to all English citizens.

common law *a system of law based on accepted customs, traditions, and past decisions*

The *Magna Carta*. The expansion of royal power in England did not go unopposed. The king's barons, or lords, resented the development of King Henry's court system because it took away some of their traditional powers. Traditionally, barons had their own courts where they decided what the laws were. The power struggle between the king and his barons was made worse by

12

King Henry's son, John, who placed new taxes on the barons soon after becoming king. Finally, in 1215, the barons joined together and forced King John to sign a charter that spelled out their rights. This document became known as the *Magna Carta,* or Great Charter.

To John's barons, the Magna Carta was simply a written guarantee of their traditional rights and privileges. It stated that the king could not place taxes on the barons without the consent of a group of influential barons known as the Great Council. The Magna Carta also stated that no free person could be imprisoned without a jury trial. In the 1200s, however, most English people were not free. Rather, they were serfs or peasant farmers who lived on land controlled by the king and his lords. Thus, most English people were not protected by the Magna Carta.

Despite protecting only a small portion of the British population, the Magna Carta was a major political achievement. It showed that a monarch's power could be legally limited by the citizenry.

Parliament. The creation of the Great Council and the signing of the Magna Carta were the first steps in the development of representative government in Britain. The barons who sat on the Great Council represented the interests of other barons in discussions with the king. By the late 1200s, the Council had achieved a great deal of influence. The Council demanded that the king seek its approval before making decisions. Eventually, the nobles who served on the Great Council became known as *Parliament.* The term *parliament* comes from the French word "parler," which means "to talk." The Great Council would discuss political ideas and policies and present its views to the king.

The English barons forced King John to sign the *Magna Carta* in 1215. It was one of the first documents to spell out the rights and privileges of a group of people.

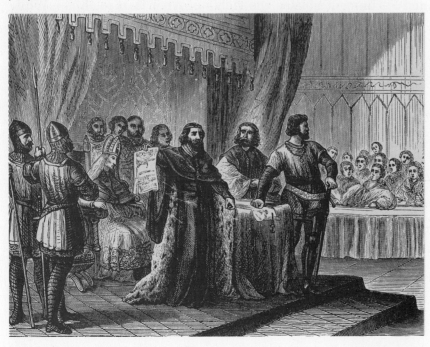

limited monarchy a government in which the rule of the king and queen is held in check by a constitution or by another part of the government

By the 1600s, Parliament had become more of an equal partner in the English government, sharing power with the monarchy. A government where a monarch does not have absolute power is a *limited monarchy*. Even though the king and Parliament shared power, they did not always cooperate with each other. James I (1603–1625) and Charles I (1625–1649), for example, claimed that they ruled by divine, or God-given, right. As a result, king and Parliament were often engaged in a bitter power struggle.

The Bill of Rights. In the mid-1600s, the power struggle between the monarchy and Parliament led to a civil war. Although Oliver Cromwell and the Puritans abolished the monarchy for 10 years, it was re-established in 1660 after Cromwell's death. In the process Parliament gained more power. By the 1680s, Parliament had so much power that it was able to pick the new queen and king to succeed King James II. Parliament offered the throne to Mary, James's oldest daughter, and her husband William. In exchange for the throne, Parliament demanded that the new queen and king sign the *Bill of Rights*.

The Bill of Rights gave the British Parliament more power than the king and queen. It stated that the monarchy could not make or suspend laws without the consent or approval of Parliament. The king and queen also needed the consent of Parliament to raise taxes and maintain an army. Finally, the Bill of Rights stated that the monarchy must not interfere in Parliamentary elections. Voters had a right to elect their representatives and the king and queen must respect voters' choices.

These three events — the signing of the Magna Carta, the creation of Parliament, and the signing of the Bill of Rights — gradually lessened the power of the British monarchy. As Parliament gained more power, the idea of the "divine right of kings" died out. The British were growing more and more interested in the idea of representative government.

The first lesson discussed ways in which the king of England and Parliament abused the rights of American colonists. While many American colonists resented these abuses, they also learned positive lessons about the value of democratic government from the British. The history of political developments in England played an important role as Americans thought about the kind of government they wanted. So did the writings of several European philosophers.

★ European Philosophers Also Influenced American Thinking on Government

During the Enlightenment in the 1600s and 1700s, many political philosophers met and discussed their ideas on government together. The Enlightenment was a period in European history when many educated people stressed the importance of learning and reasoning. Education was considered the key to understanding and solving society's problems. Many Enlightenment thinkers lived in Paris. These thinkers were known as *philosophes,* the French word for one who searches for wisdom and knowledge. Among the most influential philosophers were John Locke, Jean Jacques Rousseau, and Baron de Montesquieu.

John Locke, a seventeenth-century English philosopher, is most famous for his ideas on "inalienable rights" and the "contract theory" of government. Locke's influence on Thomas Jefferson and his writing of the Declaration of Independence is clear.

Locke Develops the "Contract Theory" of Government. John Locke, an English political philosopher, helped to further develop democratic ideas. In 1690, Locke published the *First and Second Treatises on Government*. These two books explained Locke's contract theory of government.

According to Locke, the Magna Carta and Bill of Rights protected the inalienable, or natural, rights of all British citizens. Locke wrote that all people had the inalienable "right to life, liberty, and property." Locke believed that people created government and chose to be governed in order to live in an orderly society. In other words, government arose from an agreement, or contract, between the ruler and the ruled. Thus, a ruler only had power as long as he or she had the consent of the governed. And, as a result, a ruler could not justly deny peoples' basic rights to life, liberty, and property.

Rousseau Expands the Contract Theory. In his book, *The Social Contract,* Jean Jacques Rousseau wrote about an ideal society. In this society, people would form a community and make a contract with each other, not with a ruler. People would give up some of their freedom in favor of the needs of the majority. The community would vote on all decisions, and everyone would accept the community decision. When Rousseau wrote *The Social Contract,* there was not a society in the world with such a system. His vision, however, was shared by American colonists and others.

Montesquieu Suggests Limited Government. In his book on government, *The Spirit of Laws,* Baron de Montesquieu developed practical suggestions for creating democratic governments. He stated that the best way to ensure that the government protects the natural rights of citizens is to limit its powers. And the best way to limit government's powers is to divide government's basic powers among a number of authorities.

By dividing powers between different branches or parts of the government, no one authority would have too much power. Montesquieu referred to this as a system of checks and balances.

These philosophes' ideas might sound familiar. The last lesson contained excerpts from the Declaration of Independence. In that document, recall that Thomas Jefferson wrote that "all men are created equal; that they are endowed with certain inalienable rights; that among these are life, liberty, and the pursuit of happiness." Jefferson had read Locke's Treatises very closely.

The people who created the United States Constitution found great political wisdom in the past. The system of government in place in the United States combines Ancient Greek and Roman practices with ideas developed more than 1,000 years later in Europe. Most Americans living at the time the Constitution was written were familiar with Greek democracy, the Roman republic, the British parliamentary system, and the writings of Locke, Rousseau, Montesquieu and others. The Framers of the U.S. Constitution were deeply influenced by the many ideas on government developed during the previous 2,000 years.

French political philosopher Jean Jacques Rousseau published the *Social Contract* in 1762. Many American colonists shared his vision of a community in which people made a contract with each other, not with a ruler.

Section 2 Review

1. **Defining Constitutional Terms**
   Write a brief definition for each of the following terms.

   a. democracy _____

   _____

   b. direct democracy _____

   _____

   c. citizenship _____

   _____

   d. republic _____

   _____

   e. absolute monarchy _____

   _____

   f. common law _____

   _____

   g. limited monarchy _____

   _____

2. **Reviewing Social Studies Skills:** Recognizing Cause and Effect
   Draw an arrow from the cause in the left hand list to the effect it produced in the right hand list.

   a. Enlightenment begins   Direct democracy established
   b. Poorer Athenians protest   Parliament develops
   c. English Barons rebel   New ideas about government develop
   d. Great Council created   Magna Carta is signed

3. **Reviewing the Main Ideas**
   Write a brief answer — one or two sentences — for each of the following questions.

   a. What characteristics of the American system of government reflect the influence of the

   Ancient Greeks and Romans? _____

   _____

   b. What impact did English ideas and practices have on American government? _____

   _____

   c. How did the ideas of European political philosophers influence the way the Framers wrote

   the U.S. Constitution? _____

   _____

4. **Critical Thinking Skills:** Understanding the Constitution

   On a separate piece of paper, answer the following question in a brief paragraph. How is a republic both similar to and different from the system of government known as direct democracy?

3 The Need For A New Plan Of Government

As you read, think about answers to these questions:
★ What problems did the new nation face?
★ How did the Articles of Confederation create a weak national government?
★ What caused American leaders to call for a revision of the Articles of Confederation?

The United States' first attempt to form a government, like most experiments of its kind, succeeded in some respects while failing in others. After a few years, though, the problems facing the new nation had become so serious that American leaders called for a new plan of government.

★ The New Nation Faced Several Problems

The signing of the Declaration of Independence marked the creation of a new nation. This nation was made up of 13 independent states, the 13 former colonies. Immediately, the nation faced three major problems: (1) how to fight and win the war against the British; (2) how to organize new state governments; and (3) how to develop a national government.

Fighting the Revolution. The signing of the Declaration marked the beginning of full-scale war between Americans and the British. The states and the country as a whole faced an uphill battle against Britain, then one of the most powerful nations in the world.

The struggle against Britain was made more difficult because the states had little previous experience working together. The ability to coordinate battle plans is very important in any war. The nation did not even have a real army. The state *militias* that did exist were poorly trained units and they had never worked with militias from other states. As a result, weapons were scattered across the 13 colonies, with little attention to where they would be needed most in wartime.

militias military forces that are on call for service in emergencies

Planning battle strategies requires great cooperation. In order to successfully fight a war against the British, the states needed to work together. To work together successfully, they needed a national government. Before they could create such a national government, the states needed to create their own governments.

Creating State Governments. Most states adopted written constitutions in 1776 and 1777. These constitutions set out the laws and principles of state governments. Some states simply revised their colonial *charters*. Others, such as Massachusetts, wrote new constitutions, which voters approved. The Massachusetts constitution of 1780 is the oldest written constitution currently in use anywhere in the world!

charters legal documents issued by governments to define the purpose and privileges of corporations

Despite differences between the new state constitutions, they had certain common features. The constitutions clearly spelled out the rights of citizens. Seven of the 13 documents contained a bill of rights, setting out the inalienable rights of citizens. All 13 constitutions stated, as Locke and Rousseau had, that government existed only with the consent of the governed. The constitutions also limited the power of the government by using Montesquieu's idea of separation of powers. All the states had a *legislature*, or law-making body, elected by voters. Most had a bicameral, or two-chamber, legislature made up of a senate and house of representatives. And every state except Pennsylvania had a *governor* who executed the laws. By dividing power between different branches of government, the states hoped to prevent the abuses of power the colonies had experienced under British rule.

Creating a National Government. While the states were forming their governments, the Second Continental Congress began to write a constitution for the nation as a whole. This was not an easy task. In 1776, few Americans thought of themselves as citizens of one nation. Rather, they felt loyal to their states. This loyalty had carried over from the colonial period, when each colony was practically an independent nation.

While everyone agreed that a national government was needed, the states were unwilling to give it too much power. The abuses the American colonists faced under the king of England made many Americans wary of a strong central government. This fear influenced the colonists as they decided on a new plan of government. So did the ideas about government developed in Europe during the 1600s and 1700s. Likewise, the people who were creating a new national government wanted to build on their achievements in governing the colonies prior to the 1760s.

After much debate, the delegates to the Second Continental Congress finally agreed on a new plan of government. The first constitution proposed to guide the United States government was the *Articles of Confederation*. It was completed in 1777.

The Articles of Confederation established Congress as the nation's governing body. The 13 states each agreed to send one delegate to Congress. Each state, then, had an equal vote in Congress. The Articles gave Congress several important powers including the power to declare war and to sign peace and other treaties with foreign nations. Having these powers, Congress was able to carry on with the difficult job of fighting and eventually winning the Revolutionary War.

★ **The Articles of Confederation Supported a Weak National Government**

While Americans needed a national government to carry on the war, they did not want to create another central government like the abusive British government they were fighting to overthrow. Thus, the writers of the Articles of Confederation intentionally limited the new government's powers in a number of ways.

Limited Power to Pass Laws. Although Congress was given the power to pass laws, the Articles stated that at least nine of the 13 states had to approve a law before it took effect. This weakened Congress greatly. The objections of only a few states could pre-

Money issued by the Continental Congress competed with currency printed by the 13 colonies during the American Revolution. Financial instability continued under the Articles of Confederation, creating economic confusion for the new nation.

vent important laws from being enacted even though they were desired by several states. Moreover, reaching agreements between the states was very difficult and took a long time. The states were often distrustful of each other, fearing that their interests were conflicting.

One example of how difficult it was to achieve agreements is the length of time that passed before the states actually approved the Articles of Confederation. While the Articles went into effect in 1777 — before all the states had approved them — it was not until 1781 that all 13 states voted in favor of the first U.S. constitution.

Limited Power to Tax. Congress was not given the power to tax. It could raise money only by borrowing and asking the states for funds. And the states were often unwilling to levy taxes against their citizens. This proved to be a great problem because the national government needed money to pay for the war against Britain. Congress did not even have enough money to pay army officers.

Limited Power to Regulate Trade. Congress also did not have the power to regulate or control trade between the states. The states often acted independently of each other, as if they were themselves nations. For example, states imposed *tariffs*, or taxes, on goods imported from other states. These tariffs were kept high so as to protect merchants and farmers from competitors in other states. As a result, trade relations between the states were often strained.

tariffs charges or taxes placed by the government on certain imported goods

★ Leaders Called For Revision of the Articles of Confederation

The government's inability to raise needed tax revenues and to resolve continuing trade quarrels between the states led many Americans to wonder about the value of the Articles of Confederation. The national government's lack of power was made still more evident following a rebellion in Massachusetts in 1786.

Shays' Rebellion. During the American Revolution, many farmers left their farms to fight the British. The responsibility for producing the nation's food was left in the hands of fewer farmers. Fewer farmers meant less production, increased demand, and higher food prices. In order to meet the demand, farmers borrowed money from banks for land, seed, animals, and tools. Because farm prices were up, banks were willing to lend money to farmers.

After the war, the nation suffered difficult economic times. Consequently, the prices of various goods, including farm products dropped. When crop prices fell, many farmers were suddenly unable to repay the money they had borrowed only a few years earlier.

Farmers in western Massachusetts were hard hit by falling farm prices. To make matters worse, Massachusetts raised taxes. Many farmers could not pay the taxes either. State courts began to seize the farms of people who did not pay their loans or taxes.

Daniel Shays was a Massachusetts farmer who had fought in the Revolution. In 1786, Shays gathered a force of 2,000 angry farmers. They attacked courthouses in Springfield, Massachu-

Paul Cuffee was a free black from Massachusetts. When he discovered that he did not have the same rights as white property owners, he refused to pay his taxes and went to jail in 1780. Cuffee later became a successful trader with his own fleet of ships, and he continued to fight for equal rights for black Americans throughout his lifetime.

Shays' Rebellion, in which rioting farmers attacked debt collectors and other officials, showed the weakness of the government under the Articles of Confederation. As a result of falling farm prices after the American Revolution, many farmers in western Massachusetts could not pay their taxes. When the state's courts began to seize people's farms, Captain Daniel Shays led a revolt of 2,000 angry farmers in 1786.

setts and tried to take a warehouse full of rifles and gunpowder. Massachusetts' government quickly raised an army and ended the rebellion.

Although Massachusetts ended the rebellion, many American leaders worried about the implications of this event. Writing about Shays' Rebellion, George Washington said, "I am mortified beyond expression that in the moment of our acknowledged independence we should by our conduct. . . render ourselves ridiculous. . . in the eyes of all Europe. We are fast verging to anarchy and confusion." Like other respected leaders, Washington feared that the Articles had given the national government too little power. The society lacked a powerful authority to provide order. Only five years after the states approved the Articles of Confederation, many Americans called for them to be revised or changed.

Planning to Revise the Articles. Some people felt that the economic problems that led to Shays' Rebellion were the result of a weak national government. True, Americans feared a strong national government. But many leaders felt that a weak national government was just as dangerous. By 1787, several political leaders openly questioned the value of the Articles of Confederation and called for their revision. Behind closed doors, however, the discussions were not about revision, but about writing a completely new plan of government.

Section 3 Review

1. Defining Constitutional Terms

Write a brief definition for each of the following terms.

a. militia _____

_____

b. charter _____

_____

c. legislature _____

_____

d. governor _____

_____

e. tariff _____

_____

2. Reviewing Social Studies Skills: Using a Primary Source

George Washington wrote the following words in 1780. Read them and in two or three sentences explain whether they show that Washington favored or opposed a stronger central government.

"I see one head gradually changing into 13. . . . I see the powers of Congress declining too fast for the consequence and respect which is due to them as a good representative body of America."

3. Reviewing the Main Ideas

Write a brief answer — one or two sentences — for each of the following questions.

a. What were some of the United States' chief problems between 1781 and 1787? _____

_____

_____

b. Why was the national government established under the Articles of Confederation a weak one? _____

_____

_____

_____

c. What circumstances led to the call for a revision of the Articles of Confederation? _____

_____

_____

_____

4. Critical Thinking Skills: Understanding the Constitution

On a separate piece of paper, answer the following question in a brief paragraph.
Why do you think the Articles of Confederation were more successful during the Revolutionary War than they were during the period of peace that followed?

New Jersey v. T. L. O.

You are in a school locker room with a friend. Your friend smokes a cigarette. A teacher smells the smoke, enters the locker room and finds you with your friend who has thrown the cigarette into a wastebasket. The teacher accuses both of you of smoking and takes you to the principal's office. The principal demands that you empty your pockets to prove you were not smoking. Is this fair? More important, is it legal?

Should school officials be required to have a warrant to search a student's property in a public school? In 1985, the Supreme Court confronted this question of the constitutional protection against search and seizure, guaranteed by the Fourth Amendment. That year it heard a case involving the search of a girl's purse in school.

In 1980, a teacher caught two 14-year-old girls smoking in a washroom at Piscataway High School in New Jersey. It was against school rules for students to smoke on school grounds. The principal talked to both girls. One admitted smoking, the other said she never smoked.

Searching Her Purse

The principal took the second girl to his office. Because she was a minor, the girl was referred to as T. L. O. — her initials — to keep her identity secret. The principal searched T. L. O.'s purse. He found cigarette rolling papers. The principal thought that having cigarette-rolling papers might indicate use of marijuana. Searching further, he found a small amount of marijuana, a pipe and several empty plastic bags. Other information in T. L. O's purse revealed that she might have been selling drugs to students.

The police and T. L. O.'s mother were notified. The police took T. L. O. and the evidence to police headquarters where she confessed to selling marijuana to other students. In juvenile court T. L. O. was declared a delinquent on the evidence found in her purse and

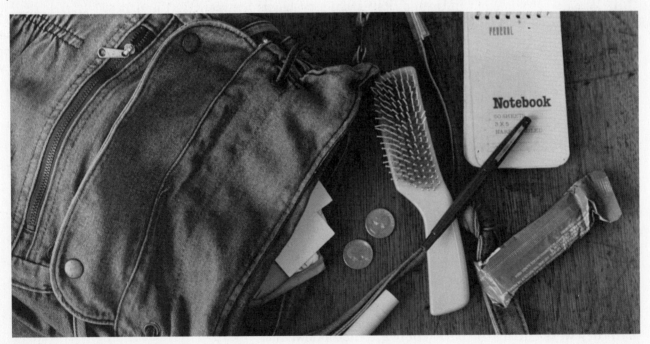

Should schools be required to have a warrant to search a student's property?

her confession. She received a year's probation, or a suspended sentence, as punishment.

T. L. O. appealed her case to the Superior Court of New Jersey. Her lawyer argued that the contents of T. L. O.'s purse should not have been presented as evidence in court. He cited the Fourth Amendment to the U. S. Constitution, which states that a warrant must be obtained before searching an individual's property. The principal had not obtained such a warrant before he searched T. L. O.'s purse.

Appealing to the U.S. Supreme Court

The Superior Court of New Jersey upheld the lower court's decision to admit the evidence. T. L. O. then appealed to the Supreme Court of New Jersey, which reversed the lower court ruling. The New Jersey Supreme Court ruled that the evidence should not have been admitted because T. L. O.'s Fourth Amendment rights had been violated; the evidence had been found illegally. The State of New Jersey then appealed to the U.S. Supreme Court.

Review the following evidence and arguments presented to the U.S. Supreme Court:

New Jersey's Arguments in Favor of Admitting the Evidence

1. School officials are not the police. They should not have to operate under the same restraints as police.
2. Teachers and principals are acting for the parents of the students. Parents do not need a warrant to search their children.
3. Schools must make the school environment one in which young people can learn. School officials need broad powers of discipline and action to do this.

4. The teacher caught the students in the act of breaking a school rule. One girl admitted breaking a rule. T. L. O. was suspected of breaking the same rule, so the principal was justified in searching her possessions. He had good reason to suspect that she broke a school rule. When he found the marijuana papers, he also had good reason to suspect that she had broken a law.

T. L. O.'s Lawyer's Arguments Against Admitting the Evidence

1. Students are entitled to the protection of the U.S. Constitution. Since the principal did not have a warrant to search T. L. O., the evidence found should not have been used against her.
2. The teachers and the principal were government agents and employees of the State of New Jersey. They are not acting as the student's parents who do have the right to search the students.
3. Students have a right to personal privacy in school.
4. The principal did not have a good reason to search T. L. O., so anything he found should not have been used against her.

Justice Byron White wrote the opinion for the majority of the Supreme Court Justices in this case. Suppose you were Justice White. What constitutional and legal issues are raised by this case? Suppose you were writing the Court's opinion. In whose favor would you decide? T. L. O.'s or the State of New Jersey's? Write your Supreme Court decision in the space below, keeping in mind the issues you have identified.

_____

_____

_____

_____

_____

_____

_____

_____

_____

_____

2 The Constitutional Convention

The Constitutional Convention met from May to September 1787.

Chapter Outline

1 Delegates' Personalities
2 Life in Philadelphia
3 Convention Proceedings and Compromises
4 Ratification

About This Chapter

On February 21, 1787, aware of its growing inability to deal with serious national problems, the Congress of the Confederation called on all 13 states to send delegates to a federal convention. The purpose of this convention was to revise the Articles of Confederation in the hope of producing a more effective national government.

Three months later, delegates from 12 states gathered in Philadelphia, at that time the largest and most exciting city in the United States. Among the most remarkable and distinguished citizens of the day, the delegates soon decided to dispense with the Articles of Confederation entirely. They set about to draft a completely new constitution. Finally, after four months of debate, disagreement, and compromise, they presented the nation with a 23-clause document. Despite its modest appearance, this document proved to be the blueprint for a new and lasting system of government.

But the delegates' work did not end with the conclusion of the Convention. Their next job was to persuade a strong and suspicious opposition to take a chance on the new constitution. Only after the hard-won approval of 11 states was secured, could the Framers rest and the United States Constitution become a reality.

1 Delegates' Personalities

As you read, think about answers to these questions:
★ Who attended the Constitutional Convention?
★ What were the delegates like as a group?
★ Who did not attend the Convention and why?
★ Who were some of the most important people at the Convention?

The states responded quickly to the Congress of the Confederation's invitation to send representatives to Philadelphia. During the spring of 1787, state legislatures chose 74 *delegates* to attend this meeting. Of that number, 55 eventually participated in what we now call the Constitutional Convention, but at the time was known as the Federal Convention. Only Rhode Island, whose political leaders were opposed to any strengthening of the national government, refused to send any delegates.

delegate a person who is authorized to act as a representative for others

★ Who Was There?

Much has been written about the remarkable collection of individuals who gathered in Philadelphia in the summer of 1787. Thomas Jefferson later referred to the delegates as "an assembly of demi-gods." By this phrase he meant to emphasize their uncommon talent and intelligence.

Had Jefferson actually been shut up in the same room with these delegates, he might have felt differently. If he had debated with them day after day during that long, hot summer, he probably would have recognized them for the earthly beings they were — beings with all the weaknesses, prejudices, and irritability of ordinary people. Jefferson's enthusiasm is, nevertheless, understandable. Seldom has so large a percentage of the distinguished and talented citizens of a nation been collected in one place. Their names — George Washington, Benjamin Franklin, James Madison, Alexander Hamilton, Roger Sherman — read like a *Who's Who* of the American Revolutionary period. They were among the most learned and experienced men of their time.

★ A Profile of the Delegates

The delegates who made the long and difficult journey to Philadelphia in May 1787, were far from typical of their nearly four million fellow Americans. At that time, about 19 out of 20 Americans lived and worked on small farms, struggling to make a modest living. By contrast the "Framers of the Constitution," as they are sometimes called, were largely wealthy and well-educated. Many of them lived in cities, and even the plantation owners among them spent more time in cities than most other Americans.

Experience and Education. The Framers were men of great public experience and prestige. Eight had signed the Declaration of Independence. Thirty had served in the Continental Army. Six had signed the Articles of Confederation. But their involvement in public life did not stop at the end of the American Revolution. Eight had already served in constitutional conventions in their own states. Seven had been or were still state governors. An astonishing 39 had been members of the Continental Congress, the Congress of the Confederation, or both. Moreover, at a time when few Americans received a higher — or any — education, 31 had attended college, including such distinguished universities as Princeton, Yale, William and Mary, Harvard, and Columbia.

Age and Occupation. Considering their experience, one of the most striking characteristics of the delegates was their youth. Only four delegates were over 60, nearly half were in their 30s, and five were less than 30. Even when Benjamin Franklin's age of 81 is taken into account, the average age of the delegates was a mere 43.

Although the Framers represented a variety of occupations, more than half were lawyers and many of those were also politicians. Apart from lawyers, merchants and plantation owners made up the largest percentage of the remaining delegates, although three were doctors, two were college presidents, and three were college professors. A majority of them were, in fact, engaged in a variety of occupations. Roger Sherman of Connecticut, for example, was not only a merchant, an almanac writer, a judge, a mayor, and a surveyor, but at one time had even been a shoemaker.

Later Service. The Framers' contributions to public life were to continue long after the Convention in Philadelphia ended. Two of them, Washington and Madison, would later be elected President and one, Elbridge Gerry, would become Vice-President. Five more served on the United States Supreme Court, two as Chief Justice. In addition, 11 would be elected state governors, 17 would serve in the Senate, and 11 would serve in the House of Representatives. It is not surprising, given these statistics, that these delegates collectively came to be known as America's "Founding Fathers."

Delegates to the Constitutional Convention often visited the home of Benjamin Franklin (seated, center) to socialize and discuss the new government.

★ Who Was Missing?

The term "Founding Fathers" immediately suggests one group that was missing from the famous gathering in Philadelphia. No women participated in the Constitutional Convention. Blacks, American Indians, and white men of modest means were also missing from the ranks of the delegates.

Groups Not Represented. While the absence of these groups might seem strange to us today, the Framers would have been equally surprised by the suggestion that they be allowed to participate. Despite the example of such remarkable and accomplished women as Abigail Adams and Mercy Otis Warren, women were viewed as dependents of their fathers or husbands. When they married, all that they owned became their husband's property. They could neither vote nor hold office.

Free blacks and American Indians also lacked political and legal rights. Even white males without property could not hold political office. Many poor and middle-income whites could not vote for the same reason.

For all their intelligence and achievements, then, the political leaders of the revolutionary generation were very much men of their time. Like their fathers, they believed that only men with property should have the right to participate fully in government. Like most white men of their generation, they saw differences in skin color and sex as signs of inferiority. Patrick Henry, famous for his fierce devotion to liberty, admitted that he would not free his slaves because of the "general inconvenience of living...without them."

Some Important Advocates of States Rights. Although the delegates argued long and hard about how much power the national government should have, many of the strongest supporters of states' rights were missing from the convention. Patrick Henry of Virginia decided early on to stay home, saying that he "smelt a rat." In other words, he believed that the convention's planners might be using the meeting to establish a powerful central government. Samuel Adams of Massachusetts, Governor George Clinton of New York and Samuel Chase of Maryland were not selected as delegates by their states. And, as mentioned earlier, Rhode Island took the drastic step of *boycotting* the convention entirely, thus giving up any influence it might have had on the final outcome.

Several Prominent Americans. Several of the better known leaders of the Revolutionary period were also missing from Philadelphia. Thomas Jefferson, author of the Declaration of Independence, was in Paris at the time, serving as minister to France. John Adams, *envoy* to England and Holland, was also out of the country. Thomas Paine was in Europe, too, trying to promote his recently invented design for an iron bridge. Jefferson and Adams did manage to exercise some influence on the convention, however, both through letters and through Adams' just-published book about constitutions.

It is impossible to tell exactly what impact all these "missing" people would have had on the writing of the Constitution. It is likely, however, that their participation would have resulted in a very different document than the one the Framers finally produced.

Abigail Adams supported women's rights. She wrote to her husband, John: "I desire you would remember the ladies, and be more generous to them than your ancestors. If particular care and attention are not paid to the ladies, we are determined to foment a rebellion, and will not hold ourselves bound to obey the laws in which we have no voice or representation."

boycott to avoid using, buying, or dealing with as a means of protest

envoy a diplomatic representative of a government

conciliator *a person who settles disputes or restores friendships*

★ Key Delegates

Some of the delegates who attended the convention in Philadelphia played more significant roles than others in the process of writing the Constitution.

George Washington. Although Washington had retired to his Mt. Vernon estate at the end of the Revolutionary War, at age 55 he was still one of the best known and most respected men in America. Over six feet tall and weighing 210 pounds, he was also a commanding figure. Washington's decision to attend the convention helped to attract other important individuals to Philadelphia. Washington did not often participate in the debate during the four-month meeting, but as president of the convention he guided the proceedings with a firm hand.

James Madison. Slight in build and balding, Madison spoke so softly that the other delegates often had to ask him to speak up. Despite his unimpressive appearance, the 36-year-old Madison contributed more to the creation of the Constitution than any other individual. Many historians now refer to him as the "Father of the Constitution." Exceptionally well educated in history and in ideas about government, he quickly became the convention's floor leader. Most of what is known of the proceedings is the result of his careful, detailed *Notes*.

Benjamin Franklin. At age 81 Franklin was the senior statesman of the convention. A writer, scientist, inventor, and diplomat, he enjoyed an international reputation. Although he was president (governor) of Pennsylvania at the time of the convention and still active in public life, Franklin's health forced him to miss many of the convention's sessions. Nevertheless, he played an important role as *conciliator* during the often heated debates.

Gouverneur Morris. Morris was only 35 in 1787. Born in New York to a wealthy family, he moved to Pennsylvania to practice law and go into business. Because of an accident, he had a wooden leg and could not use one of his arms. Yet Morris was an active participant in the convention, delivering even more speeches than Madison. A gifted writer, he was responsible for most of the actual language in the Constitution.

Alexander Hamilton. A brilliant lawyer and influential figure in New York politics, the 32-year-old Hamilton had served as Washington's secretary during the Revolutionary War. Hamilton admired the British system of government and was probably the convention's most passionate advocate of a strong national government. His desire for a single Chief Executive, chosen for life, came close to a wish for monarchy.

Of course, other delegates also made important contributions to the convention proceedings. Roger Sherman of Connecticut, William Paterson of New Jersey, and Edmund Randolph of Virginia will all be remembered for the key roles they played in the debates. Nevertheless, it is difficult to see how the meeting would have succeeded without Washington's strong presence, Madison's understanding of political and constitutional theory, or Benjamin Franklin's skills as a peacemaker. Without their participation, the Constitution might never have been written.

Section 1 Review

1. **Defining Constitutional Terms**
   Write a brief definition for each of the following terms.

   a. delegate _____

   _____

   b. boycott _____

   _____

   c. envoy _____

   _____

   d. conciliator _____

   _____

2. **Reviewing Social Studies Skills:** Reading for Historical Facts
   Write the answer to each of the following questions in the space provided.

   a. Who called for the convention to take place? _____

   b. What was the Constitutional Convention known as in 1787? _____

   c. Which two delegates later became Presidents? _____

3. **Reviewing the Main Ideas**
   Write a brief answer — one or two sentences — to each of the following questions.

   a. Who participated in the Constitutional Convention? _____

   _____

   _____

   b. How did the delegates differ from typical Americans of their time? _____

   _____

   _____

   c. What people or groups did not participate in the convention? _____

   _____

   _____

   d. Who were some of the most important delegates at the convention? _____

   _____

   _____

4. **Critical Thinking Skills:** Understanding the Constitution
   On a separate piece of paper, answer the following questions in one or two brief paragraphs.

   What impact do you think the delegates' privileged position in society had on the way they wrote the Constitution? How might the Constitution have turned out differently if some of the "missing" groups had been represented in Philadelphia?

2 Life in Philadelphia

As you read, think about answers to these questions:
★ What was Philadelphia like in 1787?
★ What were Philadelphia's strengths and weaknesses as the site of the Constitutional Convention?
★ What was memorable about the Pennsylvania State House?

hamlet a small village

In 1787 America was a nation of small farms and *hamlets*. The great majority of its citizens lived a rural existence, seldom or never visiting the country's few cities.

Against this background, Philadelphia stood out as sharply as the Framers did from their fellow Americans. With a population of 43,000 it was the largest and most *cosmopolitan* city in the United States. It was known around the country as a place of sophistication and culture.

cosmopolitan having worldwide character or sophistication

★ A Cosmopolitan City

In addition to an abundance of rooming houses, inns, taverns, and stables, Philadelphia boasted many of the features of a large

In 1787 Philadelphia was a bustling city with a population of 43,000.

European city. It had street lamps, museums, theaters, a public library, a university, numerous houses of worship, and 10 newspapers. Many of the city's streets were lined with stately brick homes.

Like any thriving, growing city, Philadelphia attracted many visitors. Newcomers to the city often commented on the variety of nations and ethnic groups represented there. Apart from sailors from many lands, French nobles, and Germans from outlying farms, one could also see frontierspeople, Quakers, American Indians, Jews, and *indentured servants* from England, Ireland, and Scotland. The city also contained a large population of free blacks.

indentured servant a person who agrees to work for another in return for travel expenses, room, and board for a set period of time

Not surprisingly, the city was a popular convention site. At the time of the Constitutional Convention, two other important groups were also meeting in Philadelphia. The governing body of the Presbyterian Church and the Society of Cincinnati, an organization composed of officers who had served in the Revolutionary War were there at the same time.

★ Site of the Constitutional Convention

There were both pluses and minuses to holding the Constitutional Convention in Philadelphia. The city was not an ideal place to spend the summer. One delegate from Maryland wrote of the upcoming Convention: "I dare not think of residing in Philadelphia during the summer." For various political and geographical reasons, however, the choice of the city made good sense.

Disadvantages. Like any rapidly growing city, Philadelphia had its share of urban problems. The city was dirty and noisy, and in many districts sanitary conditions were poor and the water unhealthy. To make matters worse, the city was famous for its intolerable summer heat, which brought with it a plague of flies and mosquitoes. One French visitor complained in his journal of the "innumerable flies which constantly light on the face and hands, stinging everywhere and turning everything black because of the filth they leave wherever they light." And even Thomas Jefferson once joked that the signers of the Declaration of Independence acted so quickly because of the flies biting through their silk stockings.

Advantages. The city had several distinct advantages as the site of the Constitutional Convention. First, it was centrally located in the country at that time, had plenty of rooming houses, and possessed a fine building in which the delegates could meet. More important, it was not New York City, home of the Congress of the Confederation and a place where the political climate was less favorable for a *radical* revision of the Articles.

radical fundamental or extreme

Conditions in the Summer of 1787. True to form, Philadelphia experienced a severe heat wave in the summer of 1787. For the purpose of secrecy, the Framers had decided at the beginning of the Convention to keep the windows in their meeting room shut. As a result, they suffered terribly in this sweltering, airless room. Noise from the street outside was also a constant problem. On at least one occasion, at the request of the delegates, Philadelphia's city commissioner had a load of gravel and hay spread over the cobblestones to cushion the noise of passing carriages.

Daily Lives of the Delegates. Most of the delegates boarded in small hotels or rooming houses. Because the delegates served at the convention without pay and paid for their own living expenses, some stayed two to a room to reduce costs.

At night delegates would meet in small groups for meals and informal discussions. These gatherings would take place in private homes or at such popular inns as the Indian Queen. During the day they would take walks or rides in the country, or would visit one of Philadelphia's many points of interest. Mr. Peale's Museum and the Delaware riverfront were two of the favorites.

Between 9:30 and 10:00 every morning, however, the delegates gathered once again at the Pennsylvania State House. There they spent much of the day debating issues and hammering out — slowly and painfully — a new constitution.

★ The Pennsylvania State House

When the Constitutional Convention opened in May 1787, the delegates gathered in the Pennsylvania State House, now known as Independence Hall. They met in the same building and the same room where the Declaration of Independence had been signed 11 years earlier.

Exterior. At the time of the Convention, many Americans maintained that the State House was the finest building on the continent. Visitors from Europe found this opinion difficult to understand. Whereas the European seats of government were often grand, impressive structures, the State House was a modest, two-story building of brick and wood. With its gabled or pitched roof and chimneys, it looked more like a fine mansion than the home of the Pennsylvania's state government.

Interior. The east chamber of the State House, where the delegates met, was a handsome, spacious room with a twenty-foot high ceiling. Two sides of the chamber were lined with wide windows, so the room was generally quite sunny. The delegates sat at tables that were covered with a green, felt-like cloth, while the presiding officer, George Washington, sat in a large, high-backed chair which closely resembled a throne. If the weather had been cooler and the windows open, it would have been a pleasant room for a meeting.

Today. The Pennsylvania State House, later renamed Independence Hall, now serves as the cornerstone of the Independence National Historical Park, one of the largest preservation efforts of historical sites ever attempted in the United States. The park was established by an act of Congress in 1948 "for the benefit of the American people." Its purpose was to restore significant historical structures "associated with the American Revolution and the founding and growth of the United States." Consisting of four city blocks in the heart of old Philadelphia, the park has witnessed the restoration of hundreds of buildings to historically accurate standards. The federal, state, and city governments, along with private groups, have combined their efforts to develop and operate the park. Among the other historical buildings in the park is Carpenters' Hall, the meeting place of the First Continental Congress.

Section 2 Review

1. **Defining Constitutional Terms**

   Write a brief definition for each of the following terms.

   a. hamlet _____

   b. cosmopolitan _____

   c. indentured servant _____

   d. radical _____

2. **Reviewing Social Studies Skills:** Making Comparisons

   a. List three urban problems that 18th-century Philadelphia and modern cities share:

   _____

   b. List three of today's urban problems that would have been unknown in 18th-century Philadelphia:

   _____

3. **Reviewing the Main Idea**

   Write a brief answer — one or two sentences — for each of the following questions.

   a. How typical was Philadelphia of American cities in 1787? _____

   _____

   _____

   b. What were some of the advantages of holding the Constitutional Convention in Philadelphia?

   _____

   _____

   _____

   c. How did the Pennsylvania State House compare with 18th-century European seats of government? _____

   _____

   _____

4. **Critical Thinking Skills:** Understanding the Constitution

   Answer the following question in a brief paragraph:

   If the Congress of the Confederation had been located in Philadelphia, would the Constitutional Convention have had more or less chance of succeeding?

   _____

   _____

   _____

   _____

   _____

3 Convention Proceedings and Compromises

As you read, think about answers to these questions:
★ What decisions did the delegates make in the opening days of the Convention?
★ In what ways was the Virginia Plan different from the New Jersey Plan?
★ Which of the compromises reached by the Convention were most important?
★ What important sources influenced the work of the delegates?
★ What final steps did delegates take to finish the Constitution?

★ The Convention Opens

The Constitutional Convention did not get off to a smooth start. Although James Madison arrived in Philadelphia a full 11 days before the Convention was scheduled to begin and George Washington arrived a day early, only a handful of delegates from two states showed up in the Pennsylvania State House on May 14. Spring rains and muddy roads delayed the arrival of many of the delegates for days.

quorum the minimum number of members who must be present for the valid transaction of business

Finally, on May 25, the Convention achieved a *quorum*. On that day 29 delegates from nine states gathered in the east chamber of the State House. They unanimously elected George Washington president of the Convention and went on to adopt several rules of procedure.

Altogether the Framers met 89 of the 116 days from May 25 through their final meeting on September 17. Of the 55 delegates who ultimately participated in the Convention, an average of 40 attended the daily sessions during those four months. The full number of 55 was not reached until August 6, when John Francis Mercer of Maryland arrived and was seated.

The Need for Secrecy. When the delegates adopted the rules of the Convention, they decided that all debates and discussion should be kept secret. Although there was criticism of this decision — from Thomas Jefferson, for one — the delegates had good reasons for agreeing to it. The Convention had already attracted much public attention and speculation. By adopting a secrecy rule, delegates hoped to protect themselves from outside pressure and insure their ability to speak their minds freely. To enforce secrecy they placed sentries at the State House doors. On the whole, the rule was well kept.

The Decision to Write a New Constitution. The Congress of the Confederation had called for a Federal Convention "for the sole and express purpose of revising the Articles of Confederation." The delegates shared a strong sense of urgency about the task ahead of them. It was clear that the Articles did not give the government the power it needed to resolve the squabbles and misunderstandings that had arisen between the states. "If no Accommodation takes place," wrote Caleb Strong of Massachusetts, "the Union itself must be dissolved."

Even before the Convention began, many of the delegates believed that more was needed than a simple revision of the Articles. James Madison had been working on an outline of a new constitution for weeks. Alexander Hamilton declared that the Articles "are fit neither for war nor peace" and that the nation "is sick and wants powerful remedies." George Washington, normally a cautious man, wrote, "My wish is that the Convention may probe the defects of the [Articles] to the bottom, and provide radical cures."

Just five days into the Convention, on May 30, the delegates adopted a proposal put forth by Edmund Randolph of Virginia. The proposal stated clearly that, rather than merely revise the Articles of Confederation, the delegates would write a completely new constitution.

On September 17, 1787, delegates from the 12 states represented at the Convention signed the new Constitution. The strong disagreements that had threatened the success of the Convention were settled by "a bundle of compromises."

★ The Virginia and New Jersey Plans

In the early weeks of the Convention, the delegates spent much of their time debating the merits of two very different proposals.

The Virginia Plan. A day before the Convention's momentous decision to create a new government, Edmund Randolph had also put forward the first plan for the new constitution. Written largely by James Madison, the "Virginia Plan" called for a new government with three separate branches: *legislative*, *executive*, and *judicial*. The plan proposed a two-house national legislature, or Congress, consisting of the House of Representatives and the Senate. Representation in both houses was to be based upon a state's population. Voters in each state would elect the members of the House of Representatives which, in turn, would choose the members of the Senate from lists of persons nominated by state legislatures.

According to the Virginia Plan, Congress would have all the powers it held under the Articles plus the power to make laws for the states, to override state laws, and to force states to obey national laws. Congress would also choose members of the judiciary and a president, who would serve for seven years.

Some delegates who feared giving too much power to a central government objected to the authority that the Virginia Plan

legislative *having the power to make laws*

executive *having the power to carry out laws*

judicial *having the power to tell what laws mean and decide if they are carried out fairly*

35

proportional representation *A system of representation based on differences in population size between areas*

gave Congress over state legislatures. The main subject of the debate, however, was *proportional representation*. Delegates from small states, such as New Jersey and Delaware, protested that this system would give larger states too much power in the national government.

The New Jersey Plan. After two weeks of debate William Patterson of New Jersey proposed an alternate plan. Like the Virginia Plan, the "New Jersey Plan" called for three branches of government and gave the central government the power to raise taxes, regulate trade, and enforce national laws.

But the plan also suggested that each state, large or small, have an equal voice in Congress, just as it had under the Articles. According to the New Jersey Plan, Congress would consist of only one house, to be elected by the state legislatures, not directly by the people. The federal executive, moreover, would include several people who would be chosen by Congress. This multi-person executive would have the power to appoint the federal judiciary.

In effect the New Jersey Plan maintained the major features of the Articles of Confederation. The Virginia Plan, on the other hand, pictured a new and more powerful national government. The delegates argued the strengths and weaknesses of these two plans for weeks. At times the debate grew heated, and several delegates on both sides of the issue threatened to withdraw. It looked for a while as if the conflict would destroy the Convention.

★ A "Bundle of Compromises"

Although the Framers debated a number of critical points, it is important to remember that they agreed on many of the basic issues they faced. The delegates were all dedicated to the concepts of *popular sovereignty* and of limited national government. Most did not question for a moment the wisdom of a representative system of government. The principles of separation of powers and of checks and balances were also accepted by a majority of delegates. Their differences, in other words, did not concern fundamental questions.

popular sovereignty *self-government based on the will of the people*

The disputes that arose were, nonetheless, serious and threatened the success of the Convention on several occasions. In the end the Constitution was born out of a series of imaginative *compromises*.

compromise *a settlement of differences in which each side gives up something*

The Great Compromise. Just when it seemed that the debate over the Virginia and New Jersey plans would bring the Convention to an end, Roger Sherman of Connecticut offered a compromise proposal to the delegates. It proved to be the central compromise of the entire Convention. The Great Compromise — or Connecticut Compromise, as it is sometimes known — proposed that the Congress should consist of two houses, a House of Representatives and a Senate. In the House, a state's representation would be based upon current population. This satisfied the heavily populated states. In the Senate each state would have two representatives. This pleased the small states.

On July 16 delegates narrowly accepted Sherman's plan. This vote not only had a lasting impact on the government of the United States, but marked a turning point in the Convention as well. The willingness to compromise on this crucial issue opened the door for other compromises.

The Three-Fifths Compromise. The acceptance of the Great Compromise immediately raised a new question for the Convention. It was a question that split northern and southern delegates: Should slaves be counted as part of the population? Southerners, who wanted to increase their representation in the House, answered yes. Northerners protested, arguing that slaves couldn't vote and shouldn't be counted.

After another long and bitter dispute, the Framers again compromised. They agreed that three-fifths of the slaves in any state would be counted in population figures. The southerners won more representation as a result of this compromise, but they also agreed that all taxes levied by Congress should be based on these figures. In short the southerners could count their slaves, but they would also have to pay for them.

Today the Three-Fifths Compromise seems curious and morally troubling to most people. Through it the Framers seemed to be giving their indirect approval of slavery. They also seemed to be saying that a black person was only worth "three-fifths" of a white person. The compromise was removed from the Constitution with the passage of the Thirteenth Amendment, which abolished slavery, in 1865.

The Commerce and Slave Trade Compromise. The South's economy was more dependent on the export of agricultural products than the North's. Consequently, southern delegates worried that northern business interests would try to hurt the interests of the agricultural South. Before they would agree to give the national government the power to control national and international trade, southerners insisted that Congress be forbidden the authority to tax the export goods of any state.

The southern delegates also argued that the slave trade was a crucial element of their region's economy. By contrast many northerners wished to abolish it completely. According to the compromise the delegates finally worked out, Congress could not abolish the slave trade for a period of at least 20 years after the Constitution went into effect.

Other Compromises. Although the above three compromises were the most significant in the making of the Constitution, there were many others. As a result, some historians have called the Constitution a "bundle of compromises." Or as Benjamin Franklin said, the delegates spent much of their time "sawing boards to make them fit." Many sections of the Constitution — those dealing with the selection of the president, the treaty-making process, the structure of the national court system, and the amendment process — all took their final form as a product of give-and-take among the Framers. Without compromises these issues could never have been resolved.

★ **Sources of the Constitution**

The Framers did not create the Constitution out of thin air. Well educated and widely read, they were familiar with the governments of Greece and Rome, as well as those of contemporary

"If men were angels," James Madison wrote, "no government would be necessary." Madison played a key role in planning the new government and making the Constitutional Convention a success.

England and Europe. As discussed in Chapter One, they also knew the political writings of their time, including Baron de Montesquieu's *The Spirit of the Law,* Jean Jacques Rousseau's *Social Contract,* and John Locke's *Two Treatises of Civil Government.*

Even more important, perhaps, was the Framers' own colonial experiences. Many of them had stood behind the *Declaration of Independence* and helped shape the Articles of Confederation and their own state governments. Some of what went into the Constitution came directly, sometimes word for word, from the Articles. A number of provisions were also drawn from various state constitutions.

★ The Convention Completes Its Work

On August 6 the delegates asked a Committee of Detail to assemble the various resolutions they had passed. During the next month this group produced a document of 23 clauses. Then the Committee on Style, headed by Gouverneur Morris, put the Constitution into its final, clear, concise form.

The delegates assembled in the State House for the last time on September 17. Few were completely happy with the document they had worked so hard to create. Many probably agreed with Benjamin Franklin, who pledged his support with these words:

> Mr. President, I confess that there are several parts of this Constitution which I do not at present approve, but I am not sure I shall never approve them: For having lived long, I have experienced many instances of being obliged by better information or fuller consideration, to change opinions, even on important subjects, which I once thought right, but found to be otherwise. It is, therefore, that the older I grow, the more apt I am to doubt my own judgment, and to pay more respect to the judgment of others.
>
> I cannot help expressing a wish that every member of the Convention who may still have objections to it, would with me, on this occasion doubt a little of his own infallibility — and to make manifest our unanimity, put his name on this instrument.
>
> In these sentiments, Sir, I agree to this Constitution with all its faults...

Franklin's speech may well have swayed some of the undecided delegates. Of the 41 still attending the Convention, 38 from 12 states came forward to sign the Constitution. Of the three who refused to sign — Edmund Randolph, George Mason, and Elbridge Gerry — Randolph later supported Virginia's ratification of the Constitution.

When they gathered in Philadelphia in May, most of the delegates believed that they were simply going to revise the Articles. Some, like Washington and Madison, feared that the convention might end in stalemate and failure. Yet in a few short months the delegates had set up the framework for a lasting government. Their work, however, was not over. Winning the approval of the states — perhaps an even more difficult job — still lay ahead.

Section 3 Review

1. **Defining Constitutional Terms**
   Write a brief definition for each of the following terms.

   a. quorum _____

   b. legislative _____

   c. executive _____

   d. judicial _____

   e. proportional representation _____

   f. popular sovereignty _____

   g. compromise _____

2. **Reviewing Social Studies Skills:** Putting Events in Sequence
   Rewrite the following list of events in chronological order.

   The Three-Fifths Compromise is reached.   1. _____

   The delegates sign the Constitution.   2. _____

   The New Jersey Plan is introduced.   3. _____

   The delegates decide to write a new Constitution. 4. _____

   The Virginia Plan is introduced.   5. _____

   The Great Compromise is reached.   6. _____

3. **Reviewing the Main Idea**
   Write a brief answer — one or two sentences — for each of the following questions.

   a. What important decisions did the delegates reach in the first few days of the Convention?

   _____

   b. How were the Virginia and New Jersey plans similar, and how were they different?

   _____

   c. What compromises were most crucial to the success of the Convention? _____

   _____

   d. What were some of the writings and experiences that helped the delegates create the
   Constitution? _____

   e. What did the delegates do to complete the process of writing the Constitution? _____

   _____

4. **Critical Thinking Skills:** Understanding the Constitution
   On a separate piece of paper, answer the following question in a brief paragraph.

   How would the Constitution and the system of government it created have been different if they
   had been based on the New Jersey Plan?

4 Ratification

As you read, think about answers to these questions:

★ How did the Federalists and Anti-Federalists view the new Constitution?

★ Which states contained the strongest opposition to the Constitution?

★ What were the first acts of the new government?

ratify to give formal approval

censure to express disapproval

The *Federalist Papers* were a series of newspaper articles written by James Madison, Alexander Hamilton, and John Jay. These articles persuaded many undecided delegates at the New York ratifying convention to vote in favor of the Constitution.

THE

FEDERALIST:

ADDRESSED TO THE

PEOPLE OF THE STATE OF
NEW-YORK.

NUMBER I.

Introduction.

AFTER an unequivocal experience of the ineffi-
cacy of the subsisting federal government, you
are called upon to deliberate on a new constitution for
the United States of America. The subject speaks its
own importance; comprehending in its consequences,
nothing less than the existence of the UNION, the
safety and welfare of the parts of which it is composed, the fate of an empire, in many respects, the
most interesting in the world. It has been frequently
remarked, that it seems to have been reserved to the
people of this country, by their conduct and example,
to decide the important question, whether societies of
men are really capable or not, of establishing good
government from reflection and choice, or whether
they are forever destined to depend, for their political
constitutions, on accident and force. If there be any
truth in the remark, the crisis, at which we are arrived,
may with propriety be regarded as the æra in which
A   that

★ Drawing the Battle Lines

The delegates in Philadelphia knew that getting the states to *ratify* the new Constitution would not be easy. The initial reaction of some representatives in the Congress of the Confederation confirmed their fears. A group of these representatives offered a resolution to *censure* the Convention for going beyond Congress' instructions to revise the Articles of Confederation. After a brief debate this motion was defeated, and on September 28 Congress submitted the new document to the states for their consideration.

Procedures. Foreseeing the strong opposition to the new Constitution, the Framers wisely decided to set up a process that would improve its chances of ratification. Rather than sending it to state legislatures, the delegates asked that it be sent to state constitutional conventions for approval. The voters in each state would elect representatives to serve in these conventions. This plan guaranteed that the people would decide the fate of the Constitution rather than state governments that had an interest in keeping power for themselves.

In Article VII of the Constitution the Framers also provided that "the ratification of the conventions of nine States shall be sufficient for the establishment of this Constitution between the States . . ." This provision greatly improved the odds of the new Constitution's being approved. Thus one or two states could not block the formation of a new government.

The Federalists. As soon as the Constitutional Convention had ended, a majority of the delegates went to work to ensure the ratification of the document they had produced. These leaders and other supporters of the Constitution came to be known as Federalists because of their desire for a strong national government. They stressed the weaknesses of the Articles and argued that only a new government based on the proposed Constitution would have the authority to solve the nation's many serious problems.

Among the most active and influential of the Federalists were James Madison, Alexander Hamilton, and John Jay. They wrote a series of newspaper articles designed to sway the decision of the New York ratifying convention. Now known as the *Federalist Papers,* these 85 essays answered many of the objections of citizens who opposed the Constitution. They remain among the best discussions of the American system of government.

The Anti-Federalists. The opponents of the Constitution, who were known as Anti-Federalists, objected to the Constitution for many reasons. Most of them believed that the document made the

This float, symbolizing the "ship of state," appeared in a New York City parade celebrating the state's ratification of the Constitution. Alexander Hamilton, after whom the float is named, led the fight for ratification.

national government too strong and gave the President too much power. Many felt that the indirect method of electing the President and Senate removed government too far from the people. Some objected to the ratification process itself.

Perhaps the most serious criticism that the Anti-Federalists directed at the Constitution was that it lacked a bill of rights to protect citizens' individual liberties. They worried that the new government might threaten the freedoms they had just fought a revolution to protect. As a result, they strongly urged that state conventions reject the Constitution.

★ Ratifying the Constitution

Delaware became the first state to ratify the Constitution on December 7, 1787. Pennsylvania, New Jersey, Georgia, and Connecticut followed within a month. In Massachusetts, a stronghold of Anti-Federalist sentiment, the delegates were more evenly divided. After a heated debate the state convention ratified in February 1788, by a vote of 187 to 168.

Four months later, in June, New Hampshire became the ninth state to approve the blueprint for a new government. Although technically the Constitution could have gone into effect at that point, Virginia and New York had not yet voted to ratify. Without these two heavily populated and important states, the new government could not hope to succeed.

Virginia and New York. Virginia delegates James Madison and Edmund Randolph had played a crucial role in creating the Constitution. Yet among those opposed to ratification were such well-known and respected Virginia politicians as Patrick Henry, George Mason, and Richard Henry Lee. They worried that the Constitution did not contain enough safeguards to protect the individual liberties of the people. Henry went so far as to call the document "the most fatal plan that could possibly be conceived to enslave a free people."

Although George Washington was not a delegate to the ratifying convention, his strong support for ratification proved decisive. Together with Madison, he was able to sway a reluctant Thomas Jefferson and several other wavering delegates. Even so, the margin of approval was only 89 to 79.

When the New York convention first convened, fully two thirds of the delegates, led by Anti-Federalist Governor George Clinton, opposed the Constitution. Fortunately, Hamilton and other supporters of the document were able to delay the convention's final vote for several weeks. During this period, a number of the delegates changed their minds after reading the persuasive *Federalist Papers.* News of the votes in New Hampshire and Virginia also helped the Federalist cause. On July 26 New York ratified the Constitution by the narrow margin of three votes.

Although Rhode Island and North Carolina initially rejected the Constitution, the votes by Virginia and New York guaranteed the future of the new government. The two *dissenting* states did not approve ratification until after this government had begun to operate: North Carolina in November 1789, and Rhode Island in May 1790.

The Call for a Bill of Rights. When Massachusetts ratified the Constitution, the state convention proposed a series of amendments to guarantee citizens' rights. Several other states — including Virginia, New Hampshire, and South Carolina — based their approval of the Constitution on the condition that a bill of rights be added. Thomas Jefferson himself wrote to Madison that "a bill of rights is what the people are entitled to against every government on earth."

Without promising the addition of a bill of rights, it is possible that the Federalists might never have won their fight to ratify the Constitution. If the Constitutional Convention had included a bill of rights in the original document, the battle for ratification would have been far less difficult.

★ Forming a New Government

When New York finally ratified the Constitution, celebrations took place in cities around the country. On September 13, 1788, in its last act under the Articles, the Congress of the Confederation paved the way for its *successor.* It chose New York City as the country's capital and called for January elections.

Choosing a President and Congress. On January 7, 1789, the states that had ratified the Constitution chose presidential electors. A month later, on February 4, those electors voted. Congressional elections were also held during this period.

The new Congress convened in Federal Hall, on Wall Street, on March 4. Because it lacked a quorum, Congress could not count the electoral vote until April 6. On that day it found that George Washington had been elected President and John Adams, Vice President. Three weeks later, Washington took the oath of office as the first President of the United States.

The First Congress consisted of 59 representatives and 26 senators. One of its first moves was to pass the Judiciary Act of 1789, which established a federal judiciary.

Drafting and Ratifying the Bill of Rights. Many of the states had ratified the Constitution with the understanding that a bill of rights would be added. The First Congress passed a series of 12 amendments in 1789. Written by James Madison, the ten of these amendments that were ratified came to be known collectively as the Bill of Rights. Chapter 3 will examine the Bill of Rights in greater detail.

dissent to disagree or withhold approval

"... a bill of rights is what the people are entitled to against every government on earth."

— Thomas Jefferson

successor a person or thing that replaces or follows another

Section 4 Review

1. **Defining Constitutional Terms**
   Write a brief definition for each of the following terms.

   a. ratify _____

   b. censure _____

   c. dissent _____

   d. successor _____

2. **Reviewing Social Studies Skills:** Finding Evidence
   To answer each of the following questions, write down the *exact* sentence from the lesson that contains the answer.

   a. According to the Framers, how many states had to approve the Constitution to ratify it?

   _____

   _____

   b. What three important and influential Virginians opposed the Constitution? _____

   _____

   _____

   c. Why did the Massachusetts ratifying convention propose that a bill of rights be added to the
   Constitution? _____

   _____

   _____

3. **Reviewing the Main Idea**
   Write a brief answer — one or two sentences — for each of the following questions.

   a. What was the difference between the Federalists' and Anti-Federalists' positions on the new
   Constitution? _____

   _____

   b. In which states was the opposition to the Constitution large and well organized? _____

   _____

   c. What important actions did the First Congress take in 1789? _____

   _____

4. **Critical Thinking Skills:** Understanding the Constitution

   On a separate piece of paper, answer the following question in a brief paragraph.

   Why did the promise of a bill of rights convince many delegates at state ratifying conventions to
   vote in favor of the Constitution?

In re Gault

You are walking to school in the morning. Half-way there, you are stopped by a police officer who tells you that a house nearby was just vandalized. He also informs you that the homeowner identified the vandal, and you fit the description. In response, you explain that you know nothing about this event and are just going to school. The officer, however, doesn't believe you and tells you to get into the patrol car. The next thing you know, he is asking you a series of questions that you do not understand. Based on your answers, the police officer informs you that you are under arrest. He then proceeds to bring you down to the local jail. Is this fair? More important, is it legal?

Should minors be granted the same protection under the law as adults in court proceedings? On July 8, 1964, Gerald Gault, an Arizona resident, was taken into custody by the local sheriff's office. He and a friend had allegedly placed an obscene phone call to Mrs. Cook, a neighbor. At that time Gerald was 15 years old — a juvenile according to the law — and was on probation for another offense. What started out as just another juvenile case, however, soon developed into a series of court battles and eventually a landmark Supreme Court decision.

Gault Is Placed Under Arrest

Gerald's parents were not at home at the time of his arrest, and the sheriff's office made no attempt to inform them of his whereabouts. After his mother arrived home from work, she learned that he had been taken into custody. Mrs. Gault went to the detention center and was told what Gerald had allegedly done. A petition of delinquency was filed with the court and a juvenile court hearing was

scheduled for the next day. Such hearings are usually held to review the facts in a case. The petition, however, made no formal statement concerning Mrs. Cook's complaint and the events which led up to the request. The petition stated, instead, that Gerald was a delinquent minor and in need of court protection. It also requested that the court consider keeping Gerald in a juvenile facility after he was found delinquent. Gerald's parents were never notified of the petition or the request made to the court.

A Hearing Is Held

At the hearing, the judge questioned Gerald. He admitted dialing Mrs. Cook's number, but stated that he handed the phone to his friend. Although Gerald's mother, older brother and probation officer testified before the judge, no sworn testimony was taken under oath, and no transcripts were made. Mrs. Cook, who accused Gerald of making the obscene call, was not present. Gerald's parents were never informed that they had the right to have an attorney represent their son. After the hearing, Gerald was taken back to the detention center where he remained for three more days.

A second hearing was held a few days later, and Gerald's mother requested that Mrs. Cook be present for the court proceedings. The judge informed Mrs. Gault that Mrs. Cook was not required by law to be present. At the end of the hearing, the judge found

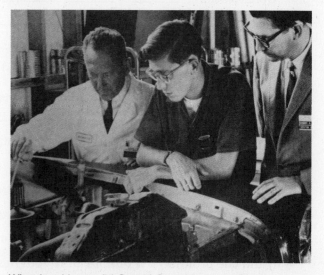

What legal issue did Gerald Gault (center) raise?

Gerald to be delinquent and sentenced him to the State Industrial School until he was 21 years old. As was the case during the first hearing, no transcripts were made, no sworn testimony was taken and no lawyer represented Gerald.

If Gerald had been 18 years of age when he committed the offense, he would have been tried as an adult in a criminal court. If found guilty, the maximum penalty would have been a fine or a two-month jail sentence. At 15 years of age, Gerald was sentenced to a maximum of six years in custody. In addition, since he was a juvenile, he did not have the legal right to appeal his sentence.

Gerald's Parents Petition for His Release

While Gerald was in the state institution, his parents filed a petition with the juvenile court requesting his release. The court denied their request. The Gaults then appealed this decision to the Arizona Supreme Court. The Arizona Supreme Court, however, agreed with the lower court's decision, upholding Gerald's conviction and sentence. Soon after, the Gaults decided to appeal their son's conviction to the U.S. Supreme Court. In 1967, the Supreme Court agreed to consider the Gault case. Because Gerald was a minor, the case was referred to as *In re Gault,* meaning "in regard to Gault."

The following arguments were presented to the Supreme Court when it heard the case:

Arizona's Arguments Against Releasing Gerald

1. The objective of a juvenile proceeding is not to convict a juvenile, but to try to correct a bad situation. The court wants to protect a child and not have the child go through the rigors of the adult criminal justice system.

2. The rights of due process are not automatically granted to juveniles.

3. When she arrived at the detention center, Mrs. Gault had been told of the charges against her son and the hearing that was to be held the next day. She didn't raise any objections at that time.

4. Gerald does not need to be represented by an attorney. His interests have been protected by his parents, the judge, and the probation officers.

Gerald's Lawyer's Arguments In Favor of His Release

1. No written notice had been given to Gerald's parents listing the charges against him.

2. Gerald had been denied his right to be represented by an attorney.

3. Gerald was never given the right to confront Mrs. Cook in court.

4. Because he was denied his right to due process under the law he lost his right to liberty.

5. Gerald had the right not to testify against himself, but was never informed of this right.

6. Due process of law had been violated in this case because there had been no transcripts made of the court proceedings.

7. Because Arizona law denied juveniles the right to appeal a case to a higher court, Gerald's right to due process had been denied.

Do minors have the right to be represented by an attorney and to confront or cross-examine those who accuse them of breaking the law? What constitutional and legal issues are raised by this case? Suppose you were writing the Court's opinion. In whose favor would you decide? The state of Arizona's or Gerald's? Write your Supreme Court decision in the space below, keeping in mind the issues you have identified.

_____

_____

_____

_____

_____

_____

_____

_____

3 The Constitution —A Living Document

Every year millions of Americans visit the National Archives
in Washington, D.C., to view the Constitution.

Chapter Outline

1 Constitutional Principles
2 The Amendment
   Process
3 Informal Changes

About This Chapter

In a 1789 letter to James Madison, Thomas Jefferson
declared, "No society can make a perpetual constitution, or
even a perpetual law." What Jefferson implied in this statement
is society's need for a "living" — or changeable — constitution.

The United States Constitution, in its original form,
contains fewer than 5,000 words. Dealing largely with matters
of basic principle, its individual sections are often brief and
undetailed. Consequently, as the Framers intended, it is open
to interpretation and change.

To insure that the Constitution would meet the needs of a
changing society, the Framers devised a formal way to amend,
or change, the Constitution. An informal process of change,
through custom and interpretation, has also helped to keep the
Constitution relevant and effective. This amendment process,
both formal and informal, has helped the Constitution to
remain a living, flexible document for more than 200 years.
As President Woodrow Wilson once observed, the Constitution
in action "is manifestly a very different thing from the
Constitution of the books."

1 Constitutional Principles

As you read, think about answers to these questions:
★ According to the Constitution, what is the source of governmental authority?
★ What does the idea of limited government mean?
★ How does the federal system divide up governmental powers?
★ What is the purpose of the separation of powers?
★ Whose power does the system of checks and balances limit?

Despite their many conflicts and disagreements, the delegates at the Constitutional Convention shared a belief in certain basic principles of government. Although the Framers did not invent these principles, they combined them in a new and original way. These principles of government reflect some of the fundamental values of our democratic system.

★ Popular Sovereignty Means the People Rule

The first underlying principle of the Constitution is the idea of popular sovereignty, or rule by the people. To understand the idea of popular sovereignty, you need only look as far as the opening words of the Constitution: "We, the people of the United States,...do ordain and establish this Constitution of the United States of America." By starting with these words, the Framers made it clear that the power of the government comes from the American people. In other words, the people are the source of all governmental power and authority. Popular sovereignty was still a revolutionary idea in the late 18th century. In fact, many of the Framers were frightened by the possibility of giving too much power to the people and encouraging mob rule.

The principle of popular sovereignty lies at the heart of the democratic principles contained in both the Declaration of Independence and the Constitution. The word *democracy* itself comes from a Greek word meaning "the people rule."

Of course, the United States has far too many people for every person to get involved in governmental decision-making. As a result, Americans elect representatives to govern them. This system of government, a republic or representative democracy, was first developed by the Romans more than 2000 years ago.

★ The Constitution Limits the Power of Government

Most of the delegates at the Constitutional Convention wished to create a stronger, more effective national government. At the same time, they were concerned that the government not become too powerful. After all, the struggle against British *tyranny* had ended just four years earlier, and the experience was still fresh in the Framers' minds.

Consequently, the delegates took steps to limit the power of the national government. The principle of limited government means that the national government does not have absolute authority. Its powers are legally limited by the Constitution.

tyranny a government in which a single ruler possesses complete power

Rule of Law. What the idea of limited government means is that government must obey the law and conduct its business according to constitutional principles. For this reason, the principle of limited government is also called the *rule of law.* No one in the government — not even Presidents or Supreme Court justices — is above the law.

The First Amendment of the Constitution begins with the words, "Congress shall make no law respecting an establishment of religion, or prohibiting the free exercise thereof . . ." Other sections of the document also restrict the power of the national government. For this reason, many scholars have concluded that the Constitution is a statement of limited government.

★ Federalism Results in a Sharing of Power

The Articles of Confederation had established a nation of nearly independent states, tied together by a weak central government. Under the Constitution, the states had to give up some of their powers to the federal government. But the states did not give up all of their powers. They reserved some for themselves.

federalism a system of government in which power is divided among national and state governments

The division of governmental authority between national and state governments is called *federalism*. One effect of the federal system is to limit the power of both national and state governments. Federalism also gives the national government the power to act for the nation as a whole, while granting states the authority to deal with local problems.

What the Federal Government Can Do. In the Constitution the Framers carefully spelled out the powers of the federal government. These include the power to coin money, regulate trade between states and foreign countries, establish a postal system, create and maintain armed forces, conduct foreign policy, and declare war. The Constitution prohibits state governments from getting involved in any of these activities. Apart from the powers they specified, the Framers also gave Congress the power to "make all laws which shall be necessary and proper for carrying into execution the foregoing powers . . ." This so-called *"Elastic Clause"* gives the Constitution greater flexibility and allows Congress to take care of the changing needs of the nation.

"Elastic Clause" constitutional power delegated to Congress, giving Congress the power to make laws needed to carry out its other responsibilities

What State Governments Can Do. The Constitution grants state governments the power to establish qualifications for voting, conduct elections, regulate trade within their borders, create local governments, and establish and maintain schools. In addition, the Tenth Amendment of the Constitution reads as follows: "The powers not delegated to the United States by the Constitution, nor prohibited by it to the states, are reserved to the states respectively, or to the people." Apart from the powers already mentioned, therefore, the states enjoy many undefined powers.

Shared Powers. The Constitution also grants a third set of powers to the federal and state governments. Among these *concurrent,* or shared, powers are the authority to build roads, enforce laws, raise taxes, and establish and maintain courts.

concurrent happening at same time or shared

The Framers realized that state governments and the federal government would sometimes disagree about who had authority in certain areas. Consequently, they indicated that the Constitution is the "supreme law of the land." When disputes arise between the federal government and state governments, the Constitution is the final authority.

★ Separation of Powers Further Limits Government

Federalism divides the power between the states and national government to prevent either from becoming too powerful. The delegates further limited the power of the federal government by dividing it into three branches. Under this system, known as the separation of powers, the legislative, executive, and judicial branches are independent of one another. James Madison explained the purpose for this division of power in the *Federalist Papers:*

> The accumulation of all powers, legislative, executive, and judiciary, in the same hands, whether one, a few, or many ... may justly be pronounced the very definition of tyranny.

Once again, the recent experience with the British made the Framers careful not to give the central government too much power.

The Congress. Congress is the legislative branch of the government. It consists of two houses: The House of Representatives and the Senate. According to Article I of the Constitution, Congress has the power to collect taxes, regulate trade between nations and states, and declare war. The main function of Congress, however, is to make laws that carry out its other powers.

The President. The executive branch of the government contains the President, the Vice President, and a variety of executive departments and presidential appointees. The President's main role, under Article II of the Constitution, is to enforce the laws that Congress passes. In addition to being the commander in chief of the armed forces, the President can propose laws, appoint federal judges, and negotiate foreign trade.

The Courts. The courts make up the judicial branch of government. Article III of the Constitution establishes a Supreme Court and gives Congress the power to set up other federal courts under the Supreme Court. The primary purpose of the federal courts is to interpret the laws and make sure they are applied fairly. The Supreme Court and federal courts hear cases that involve the Constitution, laws passed by Congress, and disputes between two or more states.

President Ronald Reagan delivers the State of the Union address to a joint session of Congress. The Constitution states that the President "shall from time to time give to the Congress information on the state of the Union. . ."

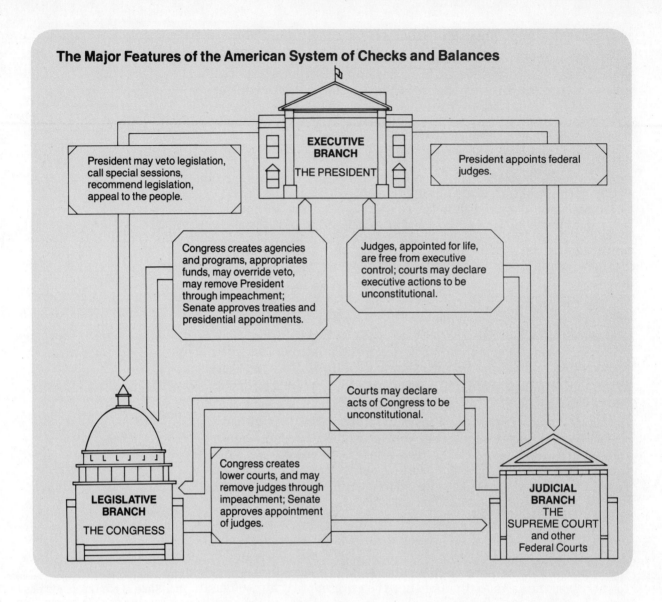

The Major Features of the American System of Checks and Balances

EXECUTIVE BRANCH
THE PRESIDENT

President may veto legislation, call special sessions, recommend legislation, appeal to the people.

President appoints federal judges.

Congress creates agencies and programs, appropriates funds, may override veto, may remove President through impeachment; Senate approves treaties and presidential appointments.

Judges, appointed for life, are free from executive control; courts may declare executive actions to be unconstitutional.

Courts may declare acts of Congress to be unconstitutional.

Congress creates lower courts, and may remove judges through impeachment; Senate approves appointment of judges.

LEGISLATIVE BRANCH
THE CONGRESS

JUDICIAL BRANCH
THE SUPREME COURT
and other Federal Courts

★ Checks and Balances Protect Against Tyranny

To make sure that one branch of the federal government did not become too powerful, the Framers established a system of checks and balances. Under this system each branch of the government has some way to check, or control, the other two branches. The effect of this system is to strengthen the separation of powers and further limit the power of the federal government.

Legislative and Executive Checks. The delegates in Philadelphia were concerned that the Chief Executive might become too powerful. To avoid this possibility, they included several important checks on presidential power in the Constitution. For example, although the President has the power to appoint cabinet officers, federal judges, and ambassadors, the Senate must approve each of these appointments. The Senate must also approve any treaties the President negotiates with foreign nations. And Congress' authority to declare war checks the President's power as Commander in Chief of the armed forces.

Congress also has the power to remove a President from office. First, the House must *impeach*, or accuse, the President

impeach to accuse or formally charge with misconduct

50

of a serious crime. Then the Senate must convict that President by a two-thirds vote.

The Constitution also checks the power of Congress in a number of ways. Both houses must pass a bill before it goes to the President. The President may then *veto* that bill. Although Congress does have the power to *override,* or overrule, that veto, it must do so by a two-thirds vote in each house.

Both the President and Congress can check the power of the courts. The President has the power to appoint all federal judges, while the Senate must approve those appointments. Congress may also impeach judges and remove from office any who are found guilty of wrongdoing.

Judicial Review. The federal courts, in turn, can check the powers of both the President and Congress. In the cases it hears, the Supreme Court can determine whether specific laws or executive actions violate the Constitution. The Supreme Court's power to declare congressional and presidential actions unconstitutional is known as the process of judicial review. The Framers did not spell out this review process directly in the Constitution. Nevertheless, a majority of them believed that the Supreme Court had this power and that it was a basic principle of American government. Chapter Four will outline the idea of judicial review in greater detail.

Checking the Power of the People. Much has been written about the Framers' fear of a tyrannical central government. It is important to remember that many of the Framers also worried that the people might abuse their power. The delegates felt that direct participation in the national government should be limited to the better educated, more privileged members of American society. Consequently, they took steps to limit the power of the people.

The delegates in Philadelphia decided that voters would choose the members of the House of Representatives directly. At the same time, they concluded that state legislatures should select members of the Senate. This indirect method of electing senators lasted until 1913, when Congress passed and the states ratified the Seventeenth Amendment. Since that date the people have elected senators directly.

The Framers also created an indirect method of electing the President and Vice President. According to the Constitution, a state must choose electors equal to the number of representatives it sends to Congress. These electors, known collectively as the Electoral College, then vote for the President and Vice President of the United States. This system of electing the President is still in effect today, though it has changed with time. Originally state legislatures chose electors. Since the middle of the nineteenth century, however, voters have chosen presidential electors directly. Customarily, electors follow the popular vote of their respective states.

Without compromise the Constitutional Convention in Philadelphia would have failed. The system of checks and balances, which limits the power of any one segment of our political system, makes compromise necessary. As a result, compromise has continued to play a vital role in our democratic system of government, just as it did in the Convention that created that system.

veto to reject or prevent a legislative bill from becoming law

override to rule against or declare invalid

Section 1 Review

1. **Defining Constitutional Terms**
   Write a brief definition for each of the following terms.

   a. tyranny _____

   b. federalism _____

   c. concurrent _____

   d. impeach _____

   e. veto _____

   f. override _____

   g. "Elastic Clause" _____

2. **Reviewing Social Studies Skills:** Distinguishing Facts Accurately

   The verbs in the right-hand column describe powers delegated to the three branches of government. Draw lines from each branch of government to the two verbs that describe its powers.

The Congress	veto
The President	interpret
	impeach
The Supreme Court	review
	override
	appoint

3. **Reviewing the Main Ideas**
   Write a brief answer — one or two sentences — for each of the following questions.

   a. What is the source of power in our governmental system? _____

   _____

   b. In what sense is the Constitution a statement of limited government? _____

   _____

   c. Why is the American system of government an example of federalism? _____

   _____

   d. Why did the Framers divide governmental power among three branches of government?

   _____

   _____

   e. How does the system of checks and balances affect the way the government works? _____

   _____

   _____

4. **Critical Thinking Skills:** Understanding the Constitution

   On a separate piece of paper answer the following question in a brief paragraph.

   Federalism, the separation of powers, and the system of checks and balances all work to limit government in the United States. How might our system of government and society be different without such limitations?

2 The Amendment Process

As you read, think about answers to these questions:
- ★ How can the Constitution be formally changed?
- ★ What does the Bill of Rights protect?
- ★ Which other amendments have had a particularly significant impact on our system of government and on our lives?

The delegates in Philadelphia knew that the Constitution could not remain exactly the same forever. They realized that any constitution, however good, needed the flexibility to adjust to times and conditions they couldn't foresee. As a result, the Framers provided a formal way to *amend*, or change, the Constitution.

amend to change or add to

★ Changing the Constitution by Amendment

While recognizing the need for flexibility, the Framers wanted to guarantee that future generations would consider proposed changes in the Constitution carefully. To ensure that changes would not be made in haste, they created a complicated amendment process.

Proposing and Ratifying Amendments. Article V of the Constitution outlines two methods for proposing amendments. In the first method, two thirds of both houses of Congress can vote to propose an amendment. In the second, a special national convention, called by Congress at the request of two thirds of the state legislatures, also has the authority to propose amendments.

The Constitution provides two ways to ratify, or approve, proposed amendments as well. An amendment becomes part of the Constitution when three fourths (currently 38) of the state legislatures approve it. This method was used to adopt 26 of the Constitution's 27 amendments. In addition, special ratifying conventions in three fourths of the states also have the power to adopt amendments.

The Framers did not include a time limit in the Constitution for the ratification of amendments. The Supreme Court, however, has ruled that ratification must occur within "some reasonable time after the proposal." In recent decades, Congress has defined "reasonable length of time" as seven years. In 1979, however, the Court extended that period three years for the proposed Equal Rights Amendment.

Since 1789, representatives and senators in Congress have proposed more than 10,000 *joint resolutions* calling for amendments to the Constitution. Congress has sent 33 of these amendments to the states for their consideration. Of these 33, only 27 have been ratified. What makes this figure even more remarkable is that only 17 changes have been made since the adoption of the Bill of Rights in 1791.

joint resolutions acts proposed by both houses of Congress and used to propose constitutional amendments

In recent years the states have rejected two amendments. Proposed in 1972, the Equal Rights Amendment (ERA) fell just three votes short of ratification and finally failed in 1982. In 1978 an amendment was proposed to give the District of Columbia seats in Congress. It was ratified in only 16 states and died in 1985.

★ The Bill of Rights Guarantees Basic Freedoms

Even before the Constitution was officially adopted, many delegates at the state ratifying conventions called for changes. Most delegates demanded that some kind of bill of rights be added to the document. Without a bill of rights, Patrick Henry asked, "How will we be protected against unjust acts of government?" Many others shared his concern.

One of the new Congress' first acts in 1789 was to pass a series of ten amendments to the Constitution. Ratified in 1791, the Bill of Rights — as these amendments came to be known — protect Americans' basic freedoms against the power of the federal government. The Fourteenth Amendment, passed 77 years later, extended this protection against the power of state and local governments.

James Madison, the author of the Bill of Rights, made it clear that these ten amendments did not actually *give* Americans any rights. Madison's thinking was influenced by the ideas of the Enlightenment. Like the philosopher John Locke, he believed that certain rights — such as life, liberty, and the pursuit of happiness — are *natural*. By "natural" he meant that people were born with them and did not need a government to grant them. The only purpose of a written Bill of Rights, Madison argued, was to prevent government from taking away these *fundamental rights*.

fundamental rights basic or essential freedoms

What the Amendments Say. The First Amendment guarantees individual liberties, including freedom of religion, freedom of speech, and freedom of assembly. It also protects freedom of the press. Not surprisingly, many people have described this amendment as "the heart of America's freedom."

The next three amendments grew out of the colonists' struggle against Britain. By guaranteeing the right of the people to keep and bear arms, the Second Amendment ensures the continued existence of state armies. The Third Amendment prohibits the government from forcing citizens to keep troops in their homes. And the Fourth Amendment, sometimes called the

Women held meetings and organized demonstrations for several decades to win the vote. With the ratification of the Nineteenth Amendment in 1920, women finally won suffrage, or the right to vote, in all national and state elections.

privacy amendment, protects citizens against "unreasonable" searches of their homes and forbids seizure of their property.

Amendments five through eight concern the rights of citizens who are accused of crimes. They also grew out of the experiences of the colonists under British rule. For example, in 1732 a printer named John Peter Zenger was arrested and charged with trying to turn the people against a colonial governor. The colonial government kept Zenger in jail for nine months before bringing his case to trial. The government also denied Zenger *bail*, the money accused people give a court to gain their freedom before a trial. The Americans who demanded a Bill of Rights wanted to make sure that they did not have to repeat the experiences of Zenger.

The Fifth Amendment guarantees *due process* of law. Due process means that the government must follow a set of specific and fair rules when accusing and trying a person of a crime. The Fifth Amendment also says that people do not have to give evidence in court that might hurt them and that they cannot be tried twice for the same crime.

The Sixth Amendment guarantees citizens a jury trial in criminal cases and the right to a lawyer. The right to a jury trial in *civil* cases is contained in the Seventh Amendment. The Eighth Amendment prevents judges from setting "excessive bail" or handing out "cruel and unusual punishments."

What the Amendments Do Not Say. The final two amendments limit the powers of the federal government to those powers granted in the Constitution. The Ninth Amendment says that rights not stated in the Constitution belong to the people. Madison included this amendment to make sure that the Bill of Rights didn't restrict citizens' rights to those decribed in the document. The Tenth Amendment reserves for the states those powers that the Constitution does not delegate to the national government. This amendment reassured Anti-Federalists, those people opposed to the Constitution, that the national government would not become too powerful.

The original purpose of the Bill of Rights was to protect individual citizens from the power of the central government. The Constitution did not say anywhere that state governments had to follow these rules. With the addition of the Fourteenth Amendment, however, state and local governments have also been required to protect these basic freedoms.

Individual Rights Versus Majority Rule. The Bill of Rights is a powerful declaration of the rights of the individual. On the other hand, the United States is a democracy, and one of the basic principles of any democracy is the idea of majority rule. According to majority rule, laws are designed to do the greatest good for the greatest number of people. But when the needs of the majority conflict with individual liberties, which principle should be followed? Should a person be allowed to say or do anything, for example, even if it hurts society as a whole?

The Bill of Rights has been at the center of some of the most important and controversial Supreme Court cases in our country's history. In these cases the justices have had to struggle again and again to find the proper balance between individual liberty and majority rule.

bail *money given by accused persons to obtain their release while awaiting trial*

due process *legal proceedings carried out according to established rules and principles*

civil *relating to ordinary community life as opposed to criminal proceedings*

★ Other Amendments

The Framers would probably be pleased to know that Congress and the states have been reluctant to add many formal amendments to the Constitution. They had intentionally made it difficult to alter the document. An average of only one amendment every 12 years has been ratified since 1791, and from 1805 to 1864 no amendments were added.

The Civil War Amendments. Perhaps the most significant of the amendments ratified after the Bill of Rights are the three passed to protect the rights of former slaves. Congress proposed and the states ratified these amendments shortly after the American Civil War, also known as the War Between the States. The Thirteenth Amendment (1865) ended slavery and forbade other forms of "involuntary servitude." The Fourteenth Amendment (1868) guaranteed American citizenship and constitutional rights to all people, regardless of their race, color, national background, or religious beliefs. This amendment also contains the Due Process and Equal Protection Clauses. These clauses require the states to protect the basic rights of all citizens. The Fifteenth Amendment (1870) prohibits any restrictions on the right to vote that are based on "race, color, or previous condition of servitude." Since some southern states still found ways to limit black citizens' voting rights, Congress passed the Voting Rights Act in 1965. This act says that states may not deny any qualified voter the right to vote.

Later Amendments. The Sixteenth and Seventeenth Amendments were both added in 1913. The first of these authorizes a federal income tax. The second provides for the popular election of U.S. senators. The Eighteenth Amendment (1919) prohibited the sale and consumption of liquor, but it was repealed by the Twenty-First Amendment (1933) 14 years later. The latter is the only amendment ever ratified by state conventions rather than state legislatures. Between these two amendments came the Nineteenth Amendment (1920), which gave women the right to vote in all national elections for the first time.

Of the six amendments ratified since 1950, three deal with voting rights, and two concern the President's term of office and presidential disability and replacement. The last, the Twenty-Seventh Amendment (1992), deals with congressional pay. It also holds the record for the longest ratification: 202 years, 7 months, and 23 days. For more information on the amendments, look at the chart in this chapter and at the annotated version of the Constitution in Chapter Five.

Changing the Constitution by formal amendment is not an easy process. It is difficult to win a two-thirds vote in even one, let alone both houses of Congress. And if Congress does manage to put together the votes to propose an amendment, there is no guarantee that three quarters of the states will then choose to ratify it. Nevertheless, the relatively small number of amendments that have been added is a tribute to the farsightedness of the delegates in Philadelphia. With remarkably few changes, the document they created has shaped and guided our system of government for more than 200 years.

Franklin D. Roosevelt broke the two-term tradition when he ran for a third term in 1940. Many Americans opposed the breaking of this tradition. As a result, the Twenty-second Amendment was ratified in 1951, prohibiting a President from serving more than two full terms.

Section 2 Review

1. Defining Constitutional Terms

Write a brief definition for each of the following terms.

a. amend _____

b. joint resolutions _____

c. fundamental rights _____

d. bail _____

e. due process _____

f. civil _____

2. Reviewing Social Studies Skills: Reading a Chart

In the chart below, circle the amendments that expanded voting rights.

Amendments to the Constitution

Amendments	Subject	Year Adopted	Time Required for Ratification
1st–10th	The Bill of Rights	1791	2 years, 2 months, 20 days
11th	Immunity of States from certain suits	1795	11 months, 3 days
12th	Changes in Electoral College procedure	1804	6 months, 3 days
13th	Prohibition of slavery	1865	10 months, 3 days
14th	Citizenship, due process, and equal protection	1868	2 years, 26 days
15th	No denial of vote because of race, color, or previous condition of servitude	1870	11 months, 8 days
16th	Power of Congress to tax incomes	1913	3 years, 6 months, 22 days
17th	Direct election of U. S. Senators	1913	10 months, 26 days
18th	National (liquor) prohibition	1919	1 year, 29 days
19th	Woman suffrage	1920	1 year, 2 months, 14 days
20th	Change of dates for congressional and presidential terms	1933	10 months, 21 days
21st	Repeal of the 18th Amendment	1933	9 months, 15 days
22nd	Limit on presidential tenure	1951	3 years, 11 months, 3 days
23rd	District of Columbia electoral vote	1961	9 months, 13 days
24th	Prohibition of tax payment as a qualification to vote in federal elections	1964	1 year, 4 months, 9 days
25th	Procedures for determining presidential disability, presidential sucession, and for filling a vice presidential vacancy	1967	1 year, 7 months, 4 days
26th	Sets the minimum age for voting in all elections at 18	1971	3 months, 7 days
27th	Congressional pay	1992	202 years, 7 months, 23 days

3. Reviewing the Main Ideas

Write a brief answer — one or two sentences — for each of the following questions.

a. In what ways can the Constitution be amended?

b. What basic liberties are protected by the Bill of Rights?

c. How have the amendments passed after the Bill of Rights changed our lives?

4. Critical Thinking Skills: Understanding the Constitution

On a separate piece of paper, answer the following question in a brief paragraph:

If you had to remove one amendment from the Bill of Rights, which would it be? Why?

3 Informal Changes

As you read, think about answers to these questions:
★ How has the way the Framers wrote the Constitution affected constitutional change?
★ How have the actions of Congress and Presidents changed the Constitution?
★ What role has custom played in changing the Constitution?
★ What impact have court decisions had on the Constitution?

The Constitution of today is not the same document that the 13 states ratified in 1787. Through the process of formal amendment, Congress and the states have eliminated some words from the Framers' original creation and added new ones. Although these formal changes have had a significant impact on the Constitution, they are by no means the only method of constitutional change. Many changes have occurred informally and involved no alterations in the Constitution's actual words.

★ The Framers Used Broad Language

Much of the Constitution deals with matters of basic principle and organization of government. In a sense, the Framers merely provided the skeleton for a government — a skeleton that future Presidents, Congresses, and Supreme Courts had to flesh out. Given the general nature of the principles they discussed and the language they used, it is not surprising that important constitutional change has often taken place informally.

For example, think about the word "people" in the Constitution's opening words, "We the People of the United States..." In 1787 "people" referred to white males who owned property. Today that word means something quite different. It now includes all men and women, whether white, black, American Indian, Hispanic, or Asian, no matter how much money they have or property they own. Thus, as the American people's attitudes and beliefs have changed, so too has the definition of a word in the *preamble* of the Constitution.

preamble an introductory statement

The broad principles outlined in the Constitution have prevented the document from becoming obsolete or outmoded. The document's elastic, flexible language has left it open to new meanings as both society and people's outlooks have changed. This process of informal amendment has occurred in many ways.

★ Legislative and Executive Actions Fill in the Details

Congress and the executive branch have both played important roles in changing the Constitution. Some of these changes occurred in the first decade after the Constitution took effect. Others evolved slowly over the next 200 years.

Congress. The Framers intended that Congress fill in the details that were missing from many sections of the Constitution. For example, the "Elastic Clause" (Article 1, Section 8) states that Congress may make any laws "which shall be necessary and proper" for carrying out its specific powers. But what does "necessary and proper" really mean? Because the Framers wrote this clause in a purposefully vague way, Congress has a good deal of freedom with which to act.

The creation of the federal court system is a good illustration of this process. Article II, Section 1 of the Constitution provides for "the Supreme Court, and . . . such inferior courts as the Congress may from time to time ordain and establish." One of the first actions Congress took in 1789 was to pass the Judiciary Act. This Act established a federal court system that included three circuit courts and 13 district courts. The Act also spelled out the procedures that the federal courts had to follow in a variety of disputes. Although they are important, none of these provisions is actually contained in the Constitution.

Similarly, the Constitution's "Commerce Clause" granted Congress the power "to regulate foreign and interstate commerce [trade]." Again, it is impossible to specify exactly what "regulate" means. As a result, Congress has used this implied power interpreted to mean that it can build hydroelectric dams, prohibit racial discrimination on buses and trains, and construct the 42,000-mile interstate highway system. By passing these, and thousands of other laws, Congress has done much to define and extend its powers granted under the Constitution.

Under Article II of the Constitution, the executive branch consists of the offices of President and Vice President, as well as several unspecified executive departments. The first Congress quickly established five executive departments, headed by an attorney general, a postmaster general, and secretaries of state, treasury, and war. These department heads came to be known as the President's *cabinet*. Today the executive branch contains 14 executive departments and a large network of other agencies and offices, all of which have been created by acts of Congress.

cabinet advisory board, composed of the heads of the executive departments

The Constitution says nothing about a cabinet, yet Presidents have met with department heads since the time of George Washington.

Presidents. The way in which different Presidents have used their powers has also had an informal but significant impact on the Constitution. The Louisiana Purchase is a good example of this process. In 1803 Napoleon Bonaparte, the dictator of France, offered to sell the United States the entire Louisiana Territory. Stretching from the Mississippi River to the Rocky Mountains, the territory was as large as the United States of that time.

Napoleon's offer presented President Thomas Jefferson with a dilemma. The Constitution said nothing about how the country could buy land from a foreign country or who had the authority to do so. Jefferson himself had long argued that the government had only those powers spelled out in the Constitution. But Jefferson also realized what the purchase of the enormous territory could mean for the future of his young country.

Jefferson finally decided to base the purchase of Louisiana on his constitutional power to make treaties with foreign nations. After a long and bitter debate, Congress agreed with him and ratified the treaty with France in October, 1803. The effect of Jefferson's decision was to expand the powers of the presidency by interpreting the meaning of the Constitution broadly. The words of the Constitution remained the same, but their meaning had changed.

Presidents have expanded their powers in other areas as well. For example, the Constitution states that only Congress may declare war. It also says that the President is the commander in chief of the armed forces. Acting as commander in chief, Presidents have used armed forces abroad in combat without declarations of war on roughly 150 occasions. In the 1960s, during the Vietnam War, President Lyndon Johnson sent half a million American combat troops around the world to fight against the North Vietnamese. Although more than 50,000 of these troops lost their lives and thousands more were injured, Congress never formally declared war during this conflict.

Once again, without actually changing the Constitution, Johnson and other Presidents before him expanded the range of presidential powers. Congress became so concerned about these increased powers that it passed the War Powers Act in 1973. This act placed restrictions on the President's ability to use troops in combat situations without congressional approval. The War Powers Act has led to numerous conflicts between the President and Congress.

An executive agreement is a pact made between a President and the head of a foreign state. Many Presidents have used these agreements in recent decades to conduct foreign policy. Presidents like executive agreements because, unlike treaties, the Senate does not have to approve them. These agreements are just one more example of the executive branch amending the Constitution in an informal way.

★ Customs Shape the Constitution's Meaning

Certain customs, or ways of doing things, have developed in our governmental system over the years. These customs are, for the most part, unwritten. Nevertheless, our government officials follow them as carefully as if they were actually contained in the Constitution.

Below is a ticket to the 1892 National Convention of the Populist, or People's, Party. Although the Constitution says nothing about political parties, custom has made them an important part of our political process.

Political Parties. America's two-party political system is a good example of such customs. A *political party* is a group of people who share the same political beliefs and who seek to control the government through the winning of elections. For much of our country's history, two major parties have dominated American politics. In most elections today only two parties — the Democratic and Republican parties — have a reasonable chance of victory. The Constitution, however, does not mention political parties. George Washington spoke out against them in his 1796 Farewell Address. Like many Americans of his day, Washington worried that political parties would divide and weaken the nation. In spite of Washington's warning, political parties have played a major role in the shaping of government and its procedures since the late 1790s.

The Constitution is also silent about the *nomination* of candidates for the presidency. Since the 1830s, however, political parties have been holding special nominating conventions to do just that. Political parties have also altered the impact of the Electoral College. They have converted it into little more than a rubber stamp, or automatic approval, of the popular vote in presidential elections. Even the way Congress organizes and conducts its business can be traced to the influence of political parties.

political party an organized group of people that seeks to control government through the winning of elections and the holding of public office

nomination the process of selecting candidates to run for public office

In 1860 delegates to the Republican Convention nominated Abraham Lincoln to be their party's candidate for President. The presidential nominating process is not outlined in the Constitution. Yet the custom of a nominating convention has informally changed the American political system.

succeed *to follow after and take over rank or title*

Other Customs. The Constitution says nothing about a presidential cabinet, acting as a group to advise the President. Beginning with Washington, however, Presidents have called on the heads of their executive departments for advice. Today it is difficult to imagine our government without the cabinet. It has assumed an accepted and essential place in the executive branch of the government.

Custom also dictated for many decades that the Vice President *succeed* to the office of a President who had died. Although eight Presidents died in office between 1789 and 1963, the Constitution did not actually spell out the process of succession. Instead, the Framers said that the powers and duties of the presidency, *not* the office itself, should be transferred to the Vice President. The practice of a Vice President succeeding to the office of the presidency did not become an official part of the Constitution until the passage of the Twenty-Fifth Amendment in 1967.

Another custom not contained in the Constitution was the "no third term tradition." Presidents respected this unwritten rule for nearly 150 years. Then Franklin Roosevelt broke it when he won a third term in 1940 and a fourth term in 1944. Many people were upset by Roosevelt's failure to uphold this tradition. As a result, Congress passed and the states ratified the Twenty-Second Amendment, which limited a President to two terms in office. What had once been an informal amendment became a formal, written addition to the Constitution in 1951.

★ Court Decisions Redefine the Constitution

Perhaps no department or branch of government has had so great an impact on the Constitution as the courts. Through the process of judicial review, the federal courts and the Supreme Court decide what the general words of the Constitution actually mean. It is the courts that rule which congressional laws or presidential actions are unconstitutional and, therefore, invalid. Having observed the role it plays in continually redefining the Constitution, Woodrow Wilson once called the Supreme Court "a constitutional convention in continuous session."

Since 1789, the Supreme Court has ruled on more than 38,000 cases. Given the broad language of the Constitution, many of these cases were controversial and hotly debated. Some of them have raised an important and continuing question — the same question that Thomas Jefferson faced in 1803. Should the words of the Constitution be interpreted strictly or loosely? The justices on the Supreme Court have struggled to find the answer to this question for over 200 years. You will study this issue and the role of the courts in greater depth in the next chapter.

The process of informal constitutional change has played a key role in the development of the American system of government. Many historians feel that it has had an even greater impact on the Constitution than the formal amendment process. The Framers would probably be pleased to learn of this development. Although they could not foresee how their descendents would alter the Constitution, they intended all along that it be a living document — one that could evolve to meet society's changing needs.

Section 3 Review

1. **Defining Constitutional Terms**

   Write a brief definition for each of the following terms.

   a. preamble _____

   b. cabinet _____

   c. political party _____

   d. nomination _____

   e. succeed _____

2. **Reviewing Social Studies Skills:** Distinguishing Fact from Opinion

   Below are five statements. Depending which they are, write "fact" or "opinion" in the spaces provided at the end of these statements.

   a. The process of formal amendment is much more important than the process of informal amendment. _____

   b. Jefferson ignored the Constitution when he decided to buy the Louisiana territories.

   _____

   c. Congress passed the Judiciary Act in 1789. _____

   d. America's two-party system is almost certainly unconstitutional. _____

   e. The First Congress established five executive departments. _____

3. **Reviewing the Main Ideas**

   Write a brief answer — one or two sentences — for each of the following questions.

   a. What impact have the Constitution's broad language and general principles had on constitutional change? _____

   _____

   b. What role have Congress and the executive branch played in translating constitutional principles into practice? _____

   _____

   c. How have customs and the practices of political parties changed the Constitution?

   _____

   _____

   d. How have court decisions affected the way we interpret the Constitution today?

   _____

   _____

4. **Critical Thinking Skills:** Understanding the Constitution

   On a separate piece of paper, answer the following question in a brief paragraph:

   If the Framers had filled the Constitution with many details and specific guidelines, how would it have affected the process of informal amendment?

Tinker v. Des Moines School District

"Hey, everybody, why so glum?" you ask as you sit down with a group of friends for lunch.

"Oh, nothing," replies a friend, sliding a newspaper in front of you. "Nothing, that is, unless you were planning on getting your driver's license this year."

Your eyes quickly find the headline about halfway down the page.

Governor to introduce bill raising the legal driving age

The accompanying story explains that a vote in the state house is planned next week. State legislators appear to be evenly divided on this issue. For the rest of the day, you and your friends can talk about little else.

A number of young people in your community, including you and your friends, have very strong opinions on this issue. You plan to show your support or opposition to the bill by wearing buttons to school expressing your position.

Your school principal, however, is concerned that the buttons will start a controversy that will disrupt school. He announces a new rule forbidding students from wearing political buttons on school grounds. The school district superintendent agrees, arguing that schools are for learning and not for political demonstrations. Do you agree with the new policy banning political buttons? Why or why not? If this happened in your school how would you feel? What constitutional rights are involved?

Protesting Through a Symbolic Act

The Supreme Court of the United States faced a similar case in the 1960s regarding the First Amendment rights of young people. The Court's opinion in this case was one of the most important decisions involving the rights of minors.

The case had its origins in the mid-1960s' protests against U.S. involvement in the Vietnam War. Forms of opposition included peace marches, picketing, and burning of draft registration cards. At many demonstrations, people were arrested when the protests turned violent.

In Des Moines, Iowa, a group of local citizens decided to demonstrate their opposition to the war by wearing black armbands during the Christmas season. Their silent protest began on December 16, and was to run until New Year's day. The group also decided to fast on the first and last day of this period.

The School Administration Responds

When the principals of the local school district heard of the plan, they adopted a policy and informed the public that any student wearing an armband would be asked to remove it. If the student refused, he or she would be suspended from school.

On December 16, despite the school's regulation, a number of students including Mary Beth and John Tinker, and two of their friends, decided to wear black armbands to school in support of the protest. When they refused to remove them, they were suspended and sent home. The students were instructed not to return to school until they were willing to appear without the black armbands. The students did not return to school until after the holidays, when the silent protest period had ended.

Did Mary Beth and John Tinker have the right to wear armbands in school?

Appealing to the U.S. Supreme Court

The parents believed that their children had been denied their right to free speech and, thus, that their constitutional rights had been violated. The Iowa Civil Liberties Union agreed and filed a petition in the U.S. District Court on the students' behalf. The district court in which the case was first heard had to rule on the following issues:

1. Is the wearing of an armband a symbol of free speech protected under the First Amendment?
2. Had the students been denied their right to free speech?
3. If so, did school officials have the right to deprive students of their First Amendment rights?

On September 1, 1966, the District Court found in favor of the school officials. It agreed that an armband was a symbol of free speech. Students had been denied their right to free speech, but with just cause. The court found that the wearing of armbands could lead to disruption and that school officials had a reasonable basis for establishing the no-armband policy. The court stated:

> In this instance, however, it is the disciplined atmosphere of the classroom, not the plaintiffs' right to wear armbands on school premises, which is entitled to the protection of the law.

The Iowa Civil Liberties Union appealed the District Court decision to the United States Court of Appeals. This court divided evenly on the issues presented. Four judges were in favor of upholding the lower court's decision. Four wanted to reverse the lower court's decision and rule in favor of the families. When an appeals court is evenly divided, the lower court's position is allowed to stand.

The Civil Liberties Union then petitioned the Supreme Court to hear the case. The Court agreed to hear the case, which was argued on November 12, 1968.

The Civil Liberties Union's Arguments in Favor of Allowing the Silent Protest

1. Students wearing armbands had not interfered with the rights of other students.
2. School discipline had not been disrupted.
3. The school district had denied students their right to free speech.

The Des Moines School District's Arguments Against Allowing the Silent Protest

1. The rule was made to avoid a disruption of school discipline.
2. Schools were no place for demonstrations.
3. Controversial issues should be confined to classroom discussions.

In 1969 the Supreme Court handed down its decision on this case. What constitutional issues do you think the Court considered? Suppose you were writing the Court's opinion. In whose favor would you decide? The students' or the school district's? Write your Supreme Court decision in the space below, keeping in mind the issues you have identified.

_____
_____
_____
_____
_____
_____
_____
_____
_____
_____

4 The Supreme Court and the Constitution

The Supreme Court has made its home in this building since 1935.

Chapter Outline

About This Chapter

Every year the Supreme Court is asked to review between 5,000 and 6,000 cases. Of these, the justices decide to hear only a few hundred per term. In deciding which cases to review, the Court looks at the importance of the underlying issues to American society at a given time.

As Americans' social attitudes change, the Court's opinions may also change. Thus, issues that had been decided years before may come before the Court again, and the justices may issue a different ruling. Likewise, the Court might decide to hear a case that a previous Supreme Court had refused to hear.

The Court's term is usually nine months long, beginning the first Monday in October and lasting until some time in June. During that span, the Court periodically issues its rulings. Many Americans wait for the outcome of a case with either excitement or dread, depending on their point of view about a particular issue.

The U.S. Supreme Court plays a crucial role in American society. Over the past 200 years, the Court has issued numerous landmark decisions that have determined the meaning of the Constitution. As you will see in this chapter, the Court's rulings have sometimes changed how Americans live.

1 The Supreme Court and Judicial Review

As you read, think about answers to these questions:
★ How were the powers of the Supreme Court defined?
★ Why was the case of *Marbury* v. *Madison* so important?
★ What post-Civil War events expanded the power of the Supreme Court?

The Constitution called for the creation of a federal government with three branches or parts: a legislative, executive, and judiciary. Article 1 created Congress, the legislative, or law-making, body. Article 2 established the office of the President, who executes or carries out the laws. Article 3 created a federal court system consisting of one Supreme Court and other lower courts. The responsibility of the Supreme Court is to judge whether the laws and actions of Congress and the President are constitutional. This responsibility is known as judicial review. The term *judicial review,* however, does not appear anywhere in the Constitution. How did the judiciary gain this important power?

★ The Supreme Court's Powers Were Defined Through Interpretation

As with most aspects of the U.S. Constitution, the meaning of Article 3 was left open to interpretation. In 1789, shortly after the Constitution was ratified, the U.S. Congress passed the Judiciary Act of 1789, which established the federal court system. Congress created a Supreme Court, three circuit courts, and 13 district courts. There was one district court for each of the 13 states.

The Constitution did not specify the number of justices that could be appointed to the Supreme Court. Through the Judiciary Act, though, Congress provided for a Chief Justice and five Associate Justices. The Constitution and Congress left undefined, however, the scope of the Court's power. These powers would gradually be defined through the Court's interpretation of the Constitution in particular cases.

The first three Chief Justices had very little impact on the direction of the Supreme Court. But the fourth, John Marshall, influenced the actions of the Supreme Court in ways still felt in the United States today. Early on in Marshall's term as Chief Justice, a seemingly insignificant case came before the Supreme Court. The case, *Marbury* v. *Madison,* however, became one of the most important Supreme Court decisions in U.S. history.

★ *Marbury* v. *Madison* Helped Define The Court's Powers

In November 1800, President John Adams, a Federalist, lost his bid for re-election to Thomas Jefferson, a Republican. The Federalists also lost control of Congress in the election. For the few months before the new President and Congress took office, however, Adams and his Federalist Party still had control.

President Adams packs the courts. During these months, Adams persuaded Congress to pass a new law, the Judiciary Act of 1801. This act gave Adams the power to appoint several new federal judges. The Federalists hoped to fill the nation's courts with people who would be opposed to the policies of the in-coming Republican administration.

Adams was generally successful in this effort, appointing some 39 new judges. Adams' Secretary of State, though, failed to deliver the *commissions* appointing three new justices of the peace before Adams' term of office ended. One of the commissions was to go to William Marbury.

Madison denies Marbury's commission. When Thomas Jefferson assumed the presidency in March 1801, he learned of Adams' attempt to pack the court with Federalist judges. He also discovered the failure to deliver the remaining commissions. To prevent these Federalists from becoming judges, Jefferson instructed his Secretary of State, James Madison, to refuse the appointments. One of those refused the commission was William Marbury. In 1803, angry and frustrated, William Marbury went to the Supreme Court in an attempt to gain his post. He wanted the Court to issue a **writ of** *mandamus* forcing Madison to appoint Marbury as a judge. Marbury, of course, was attempting to play on the sympathies of the Court. The new Chief Justice, John Marshall, had been the Secretary of State who failed to deliver Marbury's commission!

The Ruling. Marbury's strategy appeared to work. In the first part of his ruling, Marshall stated that Marbury, indeed, had a right to his commission. But, more important, he explained that the Judiciary Act of 1789, by which Congress gave the Supreme Court the power to issue a writ granting Marbury his commission, was unconstitutional. In Marshall's opinion, Congress could not give the Court such a power. Only the Constitution could, and the document said nothing about the Supreme Court having the power to issue a writ of *mandamus*. Thus, the Supreme Court could not force Jefferson and Madison to appoint Marbury because it did not have the power to do so.

While Marbury never became a justice of the peace, the Court's ruling in *Marbury* v. *Madison* established a very important *precedent*. A precedent is a legal decision that serves as an example in later court cases. Chief Justice Marshall's ruling interpreted the Constitution to mean that the Supreme Court had the power of judicial review. That is, the Court had the right to review acts of Congress and the President. If the Court found that a law was unconstitutional, it could overrule the law. Marshall argued that the Constitution is the "supreme law of the land" and that the Supreme Court has the final say over the meaning of the Constitution. During his 34 years as Chief Justice, Marshall used the power of judicial review to greatly expand the influence of the Supreme Court on the national government.

★ **The Supreme Court's Power Expanded After The Civil War**

The influence of the Supreme Court on American government expanded further after the American Civil War.

commission a legal document that authorizes a person to perform official duties

writ of *mandamus* a document that mandates, or requires, a public official to perform certain duties

precedent a legal decision that serves as an example in later court cases

Ex Parte Milligan. In 1866, the Supreme Court made an important ruling in the case *Ex parte Milligan.* This case involved the question of *habeus corpus.* The phrase *Ex parte Milligan* means "on behalf of Milligan." Milligan was a northerner who supported the Confederate cause during the Civil War. He was arrested for actively fomenting, or encouraging, rebellion in Indiana. Milligan's arrest was based on a military order given by President Abraham Lincoln.

In 1861, as war broke out between the Union and Confederate armies, Lincoln suspended the **writ of *habeus corpus.*** *Habeus corpus* is a constitutional protection against unjust arrest and imprisonment. The Constitution, however, says that during wartime, the federal government can suspend *habeus corpus* and impose military rule. But it does not say whether this applies only in areas where actual fighting is going on. In *Ex parte Milligan,* the Supreme Court ruled that neither the President nor Congress has the right to suspend *habeus corpus* throughout the United States, unless the whole country is the scene of actual fighting. Milligan's conviction was overturned because he was not living in an area where fighting was going on. The Supreme Court declared that in most cases the federal government cannot establish military rule in the United States. This ruling further demonstrated that the Supreme Court assumed the responsibility and the power to judge whether acts of the President and Congress were unconstitutional.

writ of *habeus corpus* *court order requiring the government to release a prisoner unless good cause for imprisonment can be shown*

The Fourteenth Amendment. A few years later, in 1868, the Fourteenth Amendment was ratified (see Chapter 3, Section 2). By requiring states to obey the laws of the nation, the Fourteenth Amendment indirectly increased the *jurisdiction,* or authority of the Supreme Court. Since 1868, the Supreme Court has had the power to decide the constitutionality of all laws and actions of the federal government and the states.

jurisdiction authority

The motto "Equal Justice Under Law" appears above the entrance of the Supreme Court Building. The Fifth Amendment of the Constitution says that all accused persons must receive equal treatment under the law.

Section 1 Review

1. **Defining Constitutional Terms**
   Write a brief definition for each of the following terms.

   a. commissions _____

   _____

   b. writ of *mandamus* _____

   _____

   c. precedent _____

   _____

   d. writ of *habeas corpus* _____

   _____

   e. jurisdiction _____

   _____

2. **Reviewing Social Studies Skills:** Identifying the Dates of Significant Events
   Draw a line from the event in the left hand column to the date when it occurred in the right hand column.

Ex parte Milligan	1861
Fourteenth Amendment ratified	1803
Jefferson elected	1868
Marbury v. *Madison*	1866
Civil War begins	1800

3. **Reviewing the Main Ideas**
   Write a brief answer — one or two sentences — for each of the following questions.
   a. How does the Constitution describe the powers of the Supreme Court?

   _____

   _____

   b. What was the significance of the *Marbury* v. *Madison* case? _____

   _____

   _____

   c. What events took place after the Civil War that increased the power of the Supreme Court?

   _____

   _____

   _____

4. **Critical Thinking Skills:** Understanding the Constitution

   On a separate sheet of paper, answer the following question in a brief paragraph.

   If the Supreme Court did not have the power of judicial review, how would the balance of power among the three branches of government have been affected?

2 First Amendment Freedoms

As you read, think about answers to these questions:
★ How does the First Amendment protect freedom of religion?
★ What has the Court said about freedom of speech?
★ How is freedom of the press limited?

Congress shall make no law respecting an establishment of religion, or prohibiting the free exercise thereof; or abridging the freedom of speech, or of the press; or of the people peaceably to assemble, and to petition the government for a redress of grievances.

Like much of the Constitution, the First Amendment, which you have just read, is elegant in its simplicity. So much is said in so few words. But like the rest of the Constitution, the First Amendment's power and complexity go beyond the printed document. Hidden in its 42 words is a question that has no simple answer. How do you balance the rights of the individual with the needs of society?

Ever since the Bill of Rights was approved in 1791, Americans have debated the meaning of the First Amendment. Many people believe that the First Amendment gives them the right to believe, say or write whatever they choose. Others believe that an individual's actions should never endanger the rights of the majority of citizens.

Using its power of judicial review, the Supreme Court has interpreted the meaning of the First Amendment in specific situations. In so doing, the Court has tried to balance the rights of individuals and majority rule. Occasionally the Court's decisions have placed limits on individual freedom.

★ Two Clauses in the First Amendment Protect Freedom of Religion

The First Amendment has two clauses, or parts, dealing with freedom of religion. Both clauses help reinforce a basic American belief: the need to keep religious and government matters separate. While this belief may be shared, people often disagree on how much separation is necessary or how to put the idea of separation into practice. As with other constitutional issues, the Supreme Court has been called upon to provide the answer.

The Establishment Clause. The *establishment clause* states that *"Congress shall make no law respecting an establishment of religion. . . ."* This clause prohibits the government from setting up a national religion. Most of the Court's rulings on this clause have been issued over the past 50 years and have involved religion and schools.

● *Everson* v. *Board of Education* (1947). *Everson* v. *Board of Education* involved a New Jersey law that provided public funding to transport children to private, religious schools. Opponents of the law argued that by paying to bus children to religious schools, the state was violating the establishment clause of the Constitution. The Supreme Court disagreed. The Court ruled that the state

establishment clause part of the First Amendment to the Constitution prohibiting the government from setting up a national religion

law was passed to guarantee the safety of all children traveling to school. It was not, then, a violation of the First Amendment clause requiring separation of church and state.

• *McCollum* v. *Board of Education* (1948). This case involved "release time" programs in public schools. Schools in Champaign, Illinois, were releasing some students from regular classes so that they could attend religious classes. The Court decided this action was unconstitutional because the public school was allowing its classrooms to be used for private religious instruction.

• *Engel* v. *Vitale* (1962). One of the most controversial Supreme Court decisions in the 1960s involved the issue of prayer in the public schools. In *Engel* v. *Vitale,* the Court ruled on the use of a prayer in New York State schools. The New York State Board of Education had written the prayer and had allowed students to recite it on a voluntary basis. The Court voted against the practice, even though the prayer was voluntary. The majority opinion read, in part:

> It is no[t] the business of government to compose official prayers for any group of the American people to recite as part of a religious program carried on by government.

Prayer in the schools is a recurring constitutional issue and will be more fully explored in Section 5.

The Free Exercise Clause. The *free exercise clause* states that *"Congress shall make no law . . . prohibiting the free exercise there of. . . "* This clause prohibits government from interfering in Americans' free exercise of their religious beliefs. The earliest Supreme Court decisions about church-state relations involved the Court's interpretation of the free exercise clause.

• *Reynolds* v. *United States* (1879). The first free exercise case the Court decided was *Reynolds* v. *United States.* In 1870, the federal government prosecuted George Reynolds because he had two wives. Reynolds was a Mormon, and his religion allowed the practice. Federal law, however, stated that polygamy — the practice of having more than one spouse — was a crime. After his conviction, Reynolds appealed to the Supreme Court, arguing that the government had violated his right to free exercise of religion. The Court disagreed with Reynolds. While he was free to believe whatever he wanted, his actions had to conform to U.S. laws. The Court's message was clear. The government could not regulate a person's beliefs, but it could regulate his or her actions. Although freedom of religion was to be protected, it was not without limitations.

• *Wisconsin* v. *Yoder* (1972). In this case, an Amish community objected to a Wisconsin state law requiring students to attend public school. The law, explained the Amish, conflicted with their religiously based desire to remain apart from nearby communities. Although the Court ruled that the Amish had to abide by the state law, it found the law itself excessive. The Court found that the children would only have to attend school through the eighth grade. Requiring any more attendence would conflict with the Amish's ability to practice their religion and would, therefore, be in violation of the Constitution.

Why were the establishment and free exercise clauses necessary? Many of the original colonists — such as the Pilgrims and

free exercise clause part of the First Amendment to the Constitution prohibiting the government from interfering in Americans' free exercise of their religious beliefs

Puritans — came to America to escape religious persecution in their homeland or to practice their religion without interference from the government or other groups. What some found in the New World, however, was the cold reality of religious intolerance. Thus, when the Framers set about to protect rights, religious freedom headed their list.

While these two clauses limit government involvement in religious matters, they do not completely separate church and state. In fact, in certain areas, government actually takes an active role in promoting religion. For example, church-owned property and contributions made to religious organizations are not taxed by federal, state, or local governments. In addition, United States currency makes reference to God, as does the national anthem.

★ Freedom of Speech Is Not Absolute

A system of democratic government only works effectively if citizens can openly express different points of view. Some of those points of view are bound to be unpopular. By guaranteeing citizens the right to express opposing viewpoints, the First Amendment makes it possible for people to deal with the complicated issues of the day and make wise choices.

These veterans are exercising their First Amendment right of free speech. The Constitution guarantees American citizens the right to express opposing and critical viewpoints. The Supreme Court, however, has placed limits on freedom of speech in certain situations.

Like freedom of religion, however, freedom of speech is not limitless. The Supreme Court has defined speech in a way that attempts to balance individual rights against the majority of people's desire for social order.

● *Schenck* v. *United States* (1919). In 1917, the United States was at war with Germany. Thousands of Americans were being drafted for military service. Charles Schenck had written and distributed leaflets in opposition to the war and draft. His leaflet had also condemned U.S. participation in the war.

Schenck was convicted of violating the Espionage Act of 1917. Congress had passed the act to prevent Americans from disrupting its war effort. Schenck appealed his conviction to the Supreme Court, arguing that his rights to free speech and press had been violated. The Court disagreed. In writing the Court's unanimous opinion, Justice Oliver Wendell Holmes concluded:

The question in every case is whether the words used in such circumstances are of such nature as to create a clear and present danger that they will bring about the . . . evils that Congress has a right to prevent. . . When a nation is at war many things that might be said in time of peace are such a hindrance. . . that their utterance will not be endured.

Schenck was entitled to his opinion, but his expression of it was a "clear danger" to the rest of society. By urging Americans to oppose the war, Schenck was, according to Holmes, "shouting fire in a theatre and causing a panic." In short, the Supreme Court had ruled that there are limits to freedom of speech.

• *Gitlow* v. *New York* (1925). The Court upheld Schenck's conviction because his actions and speech represented a "clear and present danger" to the nation. But what if the danger to the nation were not as threatening? Could a person still say whatever he or she wanted? This was the question raised in *Gitlow* v. *New York.*

In 1925 Benjamin Gitlow was convicted of publishing a pamphlet that called for the overthrow of all government. Under New York law, such an act was illegal because it could possibly lead to social chaos. Gitlow's defense countered by saying that no "clear and present danger" existed; Gitlow's pamphlet was a philosophical statement and would never have caused a revolt. The Court did not agree and upheld the New York law. Thus, the Court established another test of free speech. Speech that had even a tendency to create evil could be found to be illegal.

★ Freedom of the Press Can Be Limited

Closely related to the issue of free speech is that of free press. As with other areas of the First Amendment, the Court has had to balance individual rights with those of the majority of society and occasionally impose limits on freedom.

• *New York Times Company* v. *Sullivan* (1964). In this case, the Court ruled that a newspaper does not have the right to commit *libel,* or to intentionally injure a person's reputation. Despite a reporter's right to free press, a newspaper does not have the legal right to knowingly publish a false story about a person.

libel intentional injury to a person's reputation

• *United States* v. *New York Times* and *Washington Post* (1971). In the early 1970s, during the Vietnam War, another important free-press case was argued before the Supreme Court. The U.S. government had sued two newspapers, the *New York Times* and the *Washington Post,* to prevent them from publishing classified documents. In its argument before the Supreme Court, the government claimed that publication of the papers would harm the national security of the United States. The two newspapers argued that they had the right to publish even classified material. In its ruling, the Supreme Court agreed with the newspapers, saying the government had not demonstrated a real threat to the nation's security.

The Supreme Court cases covered in this lesson reflect on only three of our First Amendment rights. The cases represent only a small fraction of the total number of decisions the Court has made with respect to the First Amendment. The cases presented here, however, are sufficient to show that the Court has confronted the hidden question of the First Amendment — How do you balance individual rights with the needs of society?

Section 2 Review

1. **Defining Constitutional Terms**
   Write a brief definition for each of the following terms.

   a. establishment clause _____

   _____

   b. free exercise clause _____

   _____

   _____

   c. libel _____

   _____

2. **Reviewing Social Studies Skills:** Reporting a Story
   Imagine that you are a newspaper reporter. Then write the first paragraph (three or four sentences) of a story reporting the Supreme Court's decision in the *Engel* v. *Vitale* case.

3. **Reviewing the Main Ideas**
   Write a brief answer — one or two sentences — for each of the following questions.

   a. In what two ways does the First Amendment protect freedom of religion?

   _____

   _____

   b. How does the Supreme Court define freedom of speech? _____

   _____

   c. How have Supreme Court decisions limited freedom of the press?

   _____

   _____

4. **Critical Thinking Skills:** Understanding the Constitution
   Answer the following question in a brief paragraph.

   Do you agree or disagree with the Supreme Court's decision in the *Schenck* v. *United States* case? Explain your decision.

   _____

   _____

   _____

   _____

   _____

   _____

   _____

   _____

   _____

3 Rights of the Accused

As you read, think about answers to these questions:
★ Which amendments specifically deal with the rights of the accused?
★ Why is it important that people accused of committing crimes be presumed innocent?
★ What is the difference between procedural due process and substantive due process?
★ How has the Supreme Court redefined the rights of the accused in the last 30 years?

During the past 200 years the Supreme Court has had to maintain a delicate balance. On the one hand, the Court must defend the majority's right to be protected from criminals. On the other, the Court must ensure that those accused of criminal behavior be treated equally and fairly.

★ The Bill of Rights Protects the Accused

Three Amendments — 5, 6, and 8 — were written specifically to protect the rights of individuals accused of breaking society's laws. Chapter 3 outlines their basic provisions. Based on the English common law tradition that a person is innocent unless and until proven guilty, these amendments sought to guarantee that government administer justice fairly. In other words, their purpose was to help the government control itself while it controlled the governed.

★ An Accused Person Is Innocent Until Proven Guilty

presumption of innocence the assumption that someone is innocent until proved guilty of a crime

The rights of the accused would be almost pointless if they were not based on one of the most important principles of common law: *presumption of innocence*. Under the Bill of Rights an accused person must be regarded as not guilty of any offense until the courts clearly establish that guilt.

Reasoning Behind the Principle. This common law principle is crucial to fairness. When an individual is accused of a crime, the accused and the accuser are not equal. The government has police officers, prosecutors, and other members of the criminal justice system on its side. It also represents the majority of law-abiding citizens. Against this powerful set of forces stands the accused individual.

Because a person is presumed innocent, however, the government must assume the burden of proof. That is, the government must convince an impartial jury that the accused person actually committed the crime. The individual is not required to prove innocence. All the accused person has to do is show that the government's evidence is faulty or insufficient. The jury must find the government's evidence so convincing that not even a "reasonable doubt" remains about the accused person's guilt.

Members of the jury listen carefully while an attorney questions a witness. Article 3, Section 2 of the Constitution guarantees all American citizens the right to a trial by jury.

Problems With the Principle. Presumption of innocence presents problems to a society in which crime is widespread. The government's need to prove the guilt of every accused lawbreaker beyond a reasonable doubt is a heavy burden. As a result, criminals often go unpunished or are punished less severely than they should be. For example, if the government knows that it lacks convincing evidence against an accused person, it may simply release the person without going to trial, or it may *plea bargain* in order to obtain a conviction on a less-serious charge.

Presumption of Guilt? Although presumption of innocence undoubtedly results in some lawbreakers escaping their just punishment, presumption of guilt would lead to far worse abuses of justice. Perhaps the most extreme example of presumption of guilt in American history took place during World War II. More than 100,000 American citizens of Japanese ancestry were forced to give up their homes and businesses because the government presumed they were — or might in the future be — guilty of helping Japan win the war. The Japanese Americans were moved to special camps where they were treated as prisoners and watched constantly by armed guards.

In a society that treasures individual liberty and fears unlimited governmental power, presumption of innocence is an important principle. The states included it in the Bill of Rights to protect the rights of the accused from the power of the majority.

plea bargain the process in which an accused person agrees to plead guilty to a less-serious crime

★ Due Process of Law Is Expanded

Originally the phrase "due process of law" referred only to the rules that the national government had to follow when accusing someone of a crime. Since the passage of the Fourteenth Amendment, however, the Supreme Court has expanded the meaning of the phrase.

Procedural and Substantive Due Process. Now, in addition to "procedural due process," Americans enjoy the right of "substantive due process." An unfair law that is enforced according to the rules does not violate procedural due process, but it is unconstitutional under substantive due process. As a result, the government must make sure that: (1) its laws and policies are administered fairly, and (2) its laws and policies do not violate anyone's rights.

Due Process Procedures. Procedural due process protects the rights of persons accused of crimes from the time they are arrested through the time they are found guilty or not guilty. The arrest must be based on *probable cause* — such as a police officer seeing a crime taking place — or on a warrant issued by a judge. The arrested person must be informed of his or her right to refuse to answer any questions and to have the assistance of a lawyer. The accused individual cannot be forced to confess.

Due process of law requires that a *grand jury* or *prosecutor* determine whether enough evidence exists to put the alleged criminal on trial. First, the grand jury issues an *indictment* or the prosecutor swears in an *affidavit* that enough evidence exists to convict the accused person. Then the individual charged with a crime is entitled to be informed of the charge and to receive a speedy and public trial by jury.

During the trial the prosecution must prove the defendant's guilt to an impartial jury beyond a reasonable doubt. The defendant need not testify but does have the right to question his accusers and to demand the testimony of witnesses in his favor.

If the jury finds the defendant not guilty, the accused individual cannot be tried again on the same charge. If the jury finds the person guilty, he or she may appeal the verdict to a higher court for review. The higher court has the power to reverse the earlier verdict and to order a new trial.

★ The Supreme Court Redefines the Rights of the Accused

Like other parts of the Constitution, the Amendments dealing with the rights of the accused have been redefined by the Supreme Court. In several very important cases, the Court has decided that accused persons enjoy the same constitutional protections in state courts that they have in federal courts.

Mapp* v. *Ohio. In this famous 1961 decision, the Court declared that evidence that the police obtained illegally could not be used in a state court against the person from whom it was taken. The principle involved in this case — called "the exclusionary rule" — actually had been in force in the federal courts since 1914. In 1914, the Supreme Court had said that seizing evidence by illegal means violated the Fourth Amendment.

In *Mapp* v. *Ohio,* a woman was sent to jail after being found guilty of having obscene books in her home. The police had entered her home — without a warrant and without the woman's permission — looking for gambling materials. The Supreme Court said that the police had violated the Fourth Amendment's protection against illegal searches and seizures. Therefore, the evidence gathered during the search (the books) could not be used against the woman.

Gideon* v. *Wainwright. Similarly, a 1963 decision extended the Sixth Amendment's guarantee of an attorney to the state courts. This case concerned a Florida man — Clarence Earl Gideon — who was too poor to hire a lawyer. He asked the judge to appoint a lawyer, but the judge denied his request. Forced to represent himself, Gideon was convicted of breaking into a poolroom with the intent to steal and was sentenced to five years in prison.

From his prison cell Clarence Earl Gideon filed a petition with the Supreme Court to have his case reviewed. The Court accepted his petition and, using the Fourteenth Amendment as its guide, unanimously declared in Gideon's favor. According to the Court, the accused person's Sixth Amendment right to have a lawyer — even if he or she could not afford to hire one — applied to the state courts as well. Gideon was granted a new trial, at which he had a lawyer to represent him, and he was found not guilty. As a result, every accused person now enjoys the right to a lawyer even if the government must pay the lawyer's fee.

***Miranda* v. *Arizona*.** The Supreme Court again redefined the rights of the accused in 1966, but this case did not involve an extension of federal protection to the state courts. Instead, this case concerned the accused person's right under the Fifth Amendment not to incriminate himself or herself.

The presumption of innocence puts the burden of proof on the government. Consequently, police try hard to obtain confessions from the people they arrest. A confession makes it much easier for a prosecutor to prove guilt beyond a reasonable doubt.

In the *Miranda* case, the police had not told Ernesto Miranda of his right to remain silent and to have a lawyer with him during questioning. While being questioned, Miranda confessed to charges of kidnaping and rape. His confession was later used in court to help convict him. The Supreme Court reversed Miranda's conviction, however, and established certain guidelines that police must follow before they can question suspects. According to the "Miranda Rule," suspects must be told: (1) that they have a right not to answer questions, (2) that what they tell the police can later be used against them in court, (3) that they have a right to an attorney even if they cannot afford to hire one, and (4) that they may stop police questioning at any time.

Pursuant to law, I am informing you that I am Officer _____ of the _____ Police Department. You are now in custody and charged with the following crimes, _____ and may be charged with other crimes. You have the right to remain silent, however if you say anything such can and will be used against you in a court of law. Do you understand this? _____ You have the right to talk to a lawyer before answering any questions and have a lawyer with you before and during questioning. Do you understand this? _____ If you cannot afford a lawyer, you have the right to have a free lawyer appointed for you before any questions are asked and during any questioning. This free lawyer is at no expense or cost to you. Do you understand this? _____ During questioning you may stop at any time and refuse to answer any further questions. Do you understand this? _____ Do you want a lawyer? _____ Understanding all of the above rights, are you willing to give them up and to make a statement and answer questions at this time without a lawyer being present? _____

Revised 6/1/83

A Delicate Balance. Supreme Court decisions regarding the exclusionary rule, restrictions on police questioning, and other rights of the accused have made some Americans angry. These people feel that the judicial balance has swung in favor of the law-breakers and against the majority's right to protection from criminals. As the history of the Court shows, however, the task of redefining the Constitution is a job that is never finished. In recent years the Court has handed down several rulings that favor the rights of the majority. The court will continue to seek the proper balance between the need to defend law-abiding citizens and the need to treat the accused fairly and justly.

The Miranda Rule requires law enforcement officers to inform suspects of their rights at the time of an arrest.

Section 3 Review

1. **Defining Constitutional Terms**

   Write a brief definition for each of the following terms.

   a. presumption of innocence _____

   _____

   b. plea bargain _____

   _____

   c. probable cause _____

   _____

   d. grand jury _____

   e. prosecutor _____

   f. indictment _____

   g. affidavit _____

2. **Reviewing Social Studies Skills:** Drawing Conclusions

   Answer the following question in two or three sentences.

   Based on its rulings in *Mapp* v. *Ohio* (1961), *Gideon* v. *Wainwright* (1963), and *Miranda* v. *Arizona* (1966), what conclusions can you draw about the character of the Supreme Court in the early and mid 1960s?

3. **Reviewing the Main Ideas**

   Write a brief answer — one or two sentences — for each of the following questions.

   a. Which amendments in the Bill of Rights protect the rights of the accused?

   _____

   _____

   b. Why is the presumption of innocence such an important principle in our legal system?

   _____

   _____

   c. In what ways has the Supreme Court expanded the meaning of due process of law?

   _____

   _____

   d. How have Supreme Court decisions affected the rights of the accused during the past three

   decades? _____

   _____

4. **Critical Thinking Skills:** Understanding the Constitution

   On a separate piece of paper, answer the following question in a brief paragraph.

   How would our legal system be different if an accused person had to prove his or her innocence instead of the government having to prove that person guilty?

4 Civil Rights

As you read, think about answers to these questions:
★ What role did the Supreme Court play in the struggle by blacks to win their civil rights?
★ How have other minority groups and women used the courts to defend their civil rights?

The original purpose of the Bill of Rights was to prevent the central government from abusing individual liberties. The Constitution said nothing, however, about the states having to obey these amendments. This situation continued until the passage of the Fourteenth Amendment in 1868. Section 1 of that Amendment declares:

> No State shall make or enforce any law which shall abridge the privileges or immunities of citizens of the United States; nor shall any State deprive any person of life, liberty, or property, without due process of law; nor deny to any person within its jurisdiction the equal protection of the laws.

What the Fourteenth Amendment did, in effect, was *federalize* the Bill of Rights. In its Due Process Clause, the Amendment forbids states from depriving "any" person of his or her rights in an unfair or unreasonable manner. The Equal Protection Clause, on the other hand, prohibits states from making unjust distinctions between different groups or classes of people.

federalize to bring under the authority of the national government

Like the First Amendment, the Fourteenth Amendment has sparked some of the most interesting and controversial Supreme Court cases in the country's history. Over time the Court's interpretation of the Amendment's meaning has changed. While the Amendment was originally intended to establish and protect the rights of black citizens, its application has grown with time and circumstance. Since World War I, Asian Americans, Hispanic Americans, American Indians, and women have all turned to the Fourteenth Amendment to protect their *civil rights*

civil rights basic freedoms guaranteed to citizens by the Constitution

★ Determining the Civil Rights of Black Americans

The passage of the Fourteenth Amendment did not automatically end *discrimination* against black Americans. Despite the protections of the Fourteenth Amendment, the Supreme Court continued to walk a tightrope, narrowly defining what was or was not discrimination. Not until 1954 did the Court finally use the power of the Equal Protection Clause to overturn state laws that denied blacks their basic liberties. To understand the Court's rulings on black civil rights cases, it is useful to look first at a historic pre-Civil War case.

discrimination the act of judging people on the basis of bias or prejudice

Dred Scott v. Sandford. Dred Scott was a black slave who lived with his master in the slave state of Missouri. For several years, however, he and his master lived in both the free state of Illinois and the free territory of Minnesota. When he returned to Missouri, Scott *sued* for his freedom. He claimed that his residence in Illinois and Minnesota entitled him to be free.

sue to seek justice through the legal process

The Supreme Court ruled in 1857 that Dred Scott was not an American citizen and thus had no right to sue in federal court. Chief Justice Roger Taney (pronounced Tawney) wrote that the Framers of the Constitution did not intend slaves to be included in the term "sovereign people." The Court also ruled that the Missouri Compromise was unconstitutional. Under this compromise, reached in 1820, the United States admitted Missouri as a slave state and Maine as a free state. The purpose of this agreement was to preserve the balance in Congress between free and slave states and consequently reduce the conflict between the North and South. In deciding *Dred Scott,* however, the Court said that Congress did not have the right to prevent citizens from carrying their slaves, or "property," into free territories.

The *Dred Scott* decision upheld the Southern viewpoint — that slaves were property and that Congress could not outlaw slavery in any territory. The decision not only denied blacks the most basic of civil rights — citizenship — but pushed an already divided nation one step closer to civil war. Many historians now feel that this ruling pointed out the need for changes in the Constitution. These changes were made, and *Dred Scott* overturned, with the passage of the Thirteenth Amendment in 1865.

Civil Rights Cases. In 1875, Congress passed a Civil Rights Act to ensure the federal government's authority to prevent racial discrimination. Eight years later, in the Civil Rights Cases, the Supreme Court ruled the Civil Rights Act unconstitutional. The Court agreed that, under the Fourteenth Amendment, no state could deny a black person due process of law or equal protection of the laws. But the Court said that "no State" did not mean "no person." As Associate Justice Joseph P. Bradley put it in his majority opinion, "Individual invasion of individual rights is not the subject of the amendment." In other words, individual employers or hotel owners could continue to deny black citizens their rights without fear of punishment. Because the Fourteenth Amendment did not forbid private discrimination, according to the Court, Congress could not prohibit this type of discrimination either.

At a civil rights demonstration in the early 1960s, whites and blacks joined together to protest racial discrimination. Note the reference to "Jim Crow" laws in one of the posters.

Plessy v. Ferguson. In the 1880s and 1890s many states moved to deprive blacks of their civil rights and *segregate*, or keep them apart, from whites. Northern states segregated blacks through custom and private discrimination. Southern state legislatures, on the other hand, passed a series of *"Jim Crow" laws*, named for a song used in nineteenth century blackface minstrel shows. One of these laws, an 1890 Louisiana act, required railroads to provide "separate but equal" accommodations for blacks and whites. When a black man named Homer Plessy refused to move from a seat in the white compartment of a railroad car, he was arrested. His case became the basis for *Plessy v. Ferguson.*

In an 1896 decision the Supreme Court upheld the Louisiana statute. The Court recognized that blacks were entitled to equal protection under the Fourteenth Amendment. At the same time, it asserted that a law that recognizes differences in color "has no tendency to destroy the legal equality of the two races." The Court added "if one race be inferior to the other socially," it concluded, "the Constitution of the United States cannot put them on the same plane." In other words, the Court believed that it couldn't force whites to accept blacks as their social equals.

The Supreme Court's decision in *Plessy v. Ferguson* established the idea that "separate but equal" facilities were not a denial of equal protection of the laws. Yet facilities for blacks were seldom "equal" in reality. Black schools had poor resources and badly educated teachers. Black washrooms and railroad cars were also inferior. In addition to upholding Jim Crow laws and segregation, the Court had left the door open for further racial discrimination as well. The legal segregation allowed under *Plessy* v. *Ferguson* continued for 60 years, until 1954.

Brown v. Board of Education of Topeka. Linda Carol Brown was an eight-year-old black girl who lived in Topeka, Kansas. State law required her to travel to a distant black school even though she lived just a few blocks from a white school. Many blacks felt that this law violated the Fourteenth Amendment's Equal Protection Clause. With the help of the National Association for the Advancement of Colored People (NAACP) — an organization founded in 1909 to defend black civil rights — Linda's family sued the Topeka Board of Education.

In a historic 1954 decision the Supreme Court completely reversed its ruling in *Plessy v. Ferguson.* "Separate educational facilities," the Court declared, "are inherently unequal." Adding that the idea of separate but equal "has no place in public education," the Court ordered school integration to proceed "with all deliberate speed."

The 1954 decision marked the beginning of the modern civil rights movement. The leaders of the movement, using the Fourteenth Amendment, challenged discrimination in case after case during the next decade. Many blacks and whites purposely broke segregation laws in order to challenge them in court. The Supreme Court supported them in dozens of these cases. With the passage of the Civil Rights Act of 1964 and the Voting Rights of 1965, Congress also tried to guarantee that the federal government would uphold the civil rights of black Americans. The passage of these acts can be traced directly to the Supreme Court's decision in *Brown* v. *Board of Education.*

segregate to separate people on the basis of race, class, or ethnic background

"Jim Crow" laws laws passed by southern states in the nineteenth and twentieth centuries to force the segregation of the races

★ Determining the Civil Rights of Other Minorities and Women

Blacks are not the only Americans who have suffered as a result of discrimination. Chinese Americans, Japanese Americans, Jews, American Indians, Hispanic Americans, and women have all experienced prejudice and unequal treatment at various periods of American history. Some of these groups continue to feel the effects of prejudice. Like blacks, women and minorities have turned to the Bill of Rights and the Fourteenth Amendment in an attempt to establish and protect their civil rights.

Korematsu* v. *United States. After the Japanese attack on Pearl Harbor in 1941, Japanese Americans became the target of hostility and discrimination. In 1942 defense officials labeled Japanese Americans, most of whom lived on the west coast, a "security risk." As a result, President Roosevelt and the Justice Department granted the War Department the authority to relocate thousands of these Japanese Americans.

internment confinement or imprisonment

With almost no warning the government moved Japanese Americans to isolated *internment* camps. Most had to sell their houses, businesses, and personal possessions at great losses. Fully two thirds of those evacuated were American-born citizens.

One Japanese American named Fred Korematsu refused to obey the relocation order. After he was arrested, tried, and convicted, he appealed his case to the Supreme Court. He declared that he was an American citizen and loyal to his country.

The Supreme Court upheld Korematsu's conviction in a 1944 decision. Calling the relocation program a "justifiable wartime measure," the Court declared there was not enough time to identify which Japanese Americans were loyal and which were not.

Cleveland Board of Education* v. *Le Fleur. The struggle of women for equal rights has also produced several important Supreme Court cases. In the early 1970s, for example, Jo Carol Le Fleur sued the Cleveland Board of Education. School board regulations required women teachers to take leave without pay after a specified period of pregnancy. The regulations also stated that these teachers could only return to work at the beginning of a new semester. Le Fleur believed that these rules discriminated against women.

The U.S. government moved Japanese Americans who lived on the West Coast of the United States to inland "relocation camps" during World War II. Following the Japanese attack on Pearl Harbor, many people felt that Japanese Americans threatened the nation's security.

In a 1974 decision, the Supreme Court declared that the school board regulations were unconstitutional. The Court held that these rules violated the Due Process Clause of the Fourteenth Amendment. According to a majority of the justices, the Cleveland Board of Education had no right to dictate what should be a woman's personal choice in a family matter.

Since the passage of the Fourteenth Amendment, many groups have turned to the Supreme Court to assert their equal rights. As is clear from the above cases, the Court has not always ruled in their favor. Beginning with *Brown* v. *Board of Education,* however, the tendency of the Court has been to protect and expand the civil rights of minorities. This tendency does not mean that discrimination is a problem of the past. Each year people continue to file suits claiming that their civil rights have been, in some way, violated. Invariably these people look to the Bill of Rights and the Fourteenth Amendment to defend their basic freedoms.

Section 4 Review

1. **Defining Constitutional Terms**

   Write a brief definition for each of the following terms.

   a. federalize _____

   b. civil rights _____

   c. discrimination _____

   d. sue _____

   e. segregate _____

   f. "Jim Crow" laws _____

   g. internment _____

2. **Reviewing Social Studies Skills:** Putting Events in Sequence

   Put the following Supreme Court decisions in chronological order by inserting the letters in the proper spaces at the right.

   a. *Civil Rights Cases* _____

   b. *Brown* v. *Board of Education* _____

   c. *Cleveland Board of Education* v. *Le Fleur* _____

   d. *Dred Scott* v. *Sandford* _____

   e. *Korematsu* v. *United States* _____

   f. *Plessy* v. *Ferguson* _____

3. **Reviewing the Main Ideas**

   Write a brief answer — one or two sentences — for each of the following questions.

   a. How did the Supreme Court both hurt and help black Americans in their long struggle for civil rights? _____

   _____

   b. What other Americans have turned to the Supreme Court to protect their civil rights?

   _____

   _____

4. **Critical Thinking Skills:** Understanding the Constitution

   Answer the following question in a brief paragraph: How has the Fourteenth Amendment changed American society during the past 50 years?

   _____

   _____

   _____

   _____

   _____

   _____

5 Recurring Constitutional Issues

As you read, think about answers to these questions:

★ Why has the Supreme Court held that laws calling for prayer in public schools are unconstitutional?

★ Why did the Supreme Court rule that the death penalty is not cruel and unusual punishment?

★ When are racial quotas considered a form of reverse discrimination?

★ What limits has the Supreme Court placed on a woman's right to an abortion?

★ What is the difference between judicial activism and judicial restraint?

Justitia, the Roman goddess of justice, symbolizes the need to weigh both sides of a case equally and fairly. The Supreme Court has had to consider both sides of certain recurring constitutional issues several times.

Several crucial constitutional issues seem never to be fully resolved. The Supreme Court keeps re-examining these issues in light of changing social attitudes and the possibility for social conflict. Among the recurring issues that have created the most controversy in recent years have been prayer in the schools, the death penalty, racial quotas, and abortion. Perhaps the most controversial issue of all concerns just what role the Supreme Court should play in shaping social policy.

★ The Court Ruled on Prayer in the Schools

When the Supreme Court banned the practice of voluntary school prayer in *Engle* v. *Vitale* (1962) (see Chapter 4, Section 1) the decision met with fierce opposition from government officials as well as from religious leaders. "The Supreme Court," fumed

Senator Sam Ervin, "has made God unconstitutional." The following year, the Supreme Court faced the related issue of daily Bible readings in school.

School District of Abington Township v. Schempp. The 1962 Supreme Court decision had been based on what the justices saw as an inconsistency between school prayer and the Establishment Clause of the First Amendment. This clause prohibits the government from either promoting any religion or stopping anyone from practicing the religion of his or her choice.

In 1963, another school-prayer case, the *Schempp* case, came before the Supreme Court. This case involved a challenge to a Pennsylvania law that required public schools to start each day with a reading of at least 10 verses from the Bible. At the Abington Senior High School, this reading — broadcast over the school intercom — was done by a student volunteer and was followed by students in their classrooms. They then recited the Lord's Prayer and the Pledge of Allegiance.

The Schempps, whose son was a student at the school, sued the Abington School District on the basis that the state law was unconstitutional. The required Bible reading, they claimed, violated the First Amendment's Establishment Clause. Moreover, they argued, the school favored the Christian religion over all others by supplying only a King James Bible for the readings.

The Abington School District countered the Schempp arguments by saying that no religious instruction was involved. Participation was voluntary, and students could read any portion of whatever version of the Bible they wished to bring to school.

In its 8-to-1 decision, the Supreme Court declared that the state law was a violation of the Schempps' rights. The Court said that in order not to violate the Establishment Clause a law had to have a secular or non-religious purpose. The Court held that the Pennsylvania law had a religious purpose.

Wallace v. Jaffree. More than 20 years later, the Supreme Court decided another case involving prayer in the public schools. This 1985 case involved a challenge to an Alabama law that called for a "one-minute period of silence in all public schools for meditation or voluntary prayer."

Jaffree, a resident of Mobile, argued that the law lacked a secular purpose. Its real purpose was to return prayer to the public schools. By giving state approval to prayer as an activity for students, Alabama was violating the Establishment Clause.

Lawyers for the State of Alabama — whose governor at the time was George Wallace — argued that the law did not endorse prayer but only allowed students to pray if they chose to. Since the state was not forcing any student to pray, it was maintaining the "neutrality" that earlier Court decisions had required.

In a 6-to-3 decision, the Supreme Court declared that the Alabama law violated the Establishment Clause. According to the Court majority, the law — by mentioning voluntary prayer as an acceptable student activity for the one minute of silence — endorsed prayer and did not have a secular purpose.

Since the *Wallace* decision, the Court has ruled that the offering of prayer as part of a public school graduation ceremony is unconstitutional. That decision was handed down in a 1992 Rhode Island case, *Lee* v. *Weisman*.

★ The Court Ruled on the Death Penalty

The issue of whether the death penalty violates the Eighth Amendment's ban on cruel and unusual punishment has come before the Supreme Court many times. Not until 1972, however, did the Court use the Eighth Amendment to strike down state death-penalty laws.

Furman v. Georgia. In a narrow 5-to-4 decision, the Supreme Court effectively banned the death penalty in the United States. In the 1972 case of *Furman* v. *Georgia* (and a similar case, *Branch* v. *Texas)*, the Court said that the state death-penalty laws in Georgia and Texas gave juries too much freedom to impose or not impose the death penalty. The result was random use of *capital punishment.* Justice William O. Douglas wrote in his opinion that "under these laws no standards govern the selection of the penalty. People live or die, dependent on the whim of one man or 12."

As a result of the Court's decision in *Furman* v. *Georgia,* 36 states passed new laws concerning the death penalty. The purpose of these new laws was to limit a jury's freedom in imposing the death penalty. By 1976, the Supreme Court was faced with deciding the constitutionality of these new state laws.

Proffitt v. Florida. Of the 36 states passing new death-penalty laws, several tried to avoid the Supreme Court's objections in the *Furman* case by making the death penalty mandatory, or required, for first-degree murder. A first-degree murder is one committed by a person who planned the murder ahead of time. In 1976 — by a 5-to-4 vote — the Court declared these state laws unconstitutional because they did not let a jury consider either the particular circumstances of the crime or the emotional condition of the convicted murderer.

In *Proffitt* v. *Florida,* however, the court upheld the constitutionality of death-penalty laws passed in the other states. These states set up a two-stage procedure for capital, or murder, cases. The first stage was a trial to determine guilt or innocence; the second stage was to decide whether the death penalty should be imposed. The Supreme Court said this procedure would eliminate the objections raised in the *Furman* case as long as strict guidelines were followed in imposing the death penalty.

By its ruling in *Proffitt,* the Court declared that the death penalty is not cruel and unusual punishment and, therefore, not a violation of the Eighth Amendment.

★ The Court Ruled on Racial Quotas

The Civil Rights Act of 1964 banned discrimination, or unfair treatment, based on race or color from nearly all aspects of American life. The following year, the Federal Government started requiring schools and businesses to adopt *affirmative action* programs. These programs were aimed at ending the effects of past discrimination by giving favored treatment to minority groups.

Regents of University of California v. Bakke. By favoring minority group members over whites, however, affirmative action pro-

capital punishment the death penalty

affirmative action a program aimed at ending the effects of past discrimination by giving favored treatment to minority groups

grams ran the risk of causing *reverse discrimination*. In 1978, the Supreme Court made a major ruling on affirmative action programs in the *Bakke* case.

Allan Bakke, a white student who wanted to attend medical school, was refused admission by the University of California at Davis. The university's medical school took in 100 new students each year. Of the 100 openings, 16 were reserved for members of minority groups.

Bakke sued the University of California on the basis that the medical school's affirmative action program violated his Fourteenth Amendment right to equal protection of the laws. Since Bakke had better qualifications than some of the minority students who were accepted, he argued that it was the school's *quota* system that had caused him to be rejected.

The *Bakke* case resulted in two 5-to-4 Supreme Court rulings. In the first ruling, the majority said that the university's quota system was a violation of the Civil Rights Act of 1964. Reverse discrimination was illegal in any program receiving federal funds, and therefore Allan Bakke was entitled to be accepted to the medical school.

In its second 5-to-4 ruling, on the other hand, the Supreme Court approved affirmative action programs based on race as long as no rigid quotas were involved. Belonging to a minority group could be regarded as a "plus" for the student — something like participating in an outside activity or having a special talent — that a school might consider along with grades and other qualifications.

United Steel Workers v. Weber. The following year, 1979, the Supreme Court faced another quota case based on the 1964 Civil Rights Act. But this case was different from *Bakke* in that it involved a private employer rather than a public university.

Brian Weber, a white employee of Kaiser Aluminum, sued both the company and the United Steel Workers of America when he was rejected from a training program set up by Kaiser and the union. This program reserved half of its openings for minority group members. Weber argued that the program's quota was reverse discrimination.

In a 5-to-2 decision (two justices did not participate in the case), the Supreme Court ruled that quotas aimed at ending racial discrimination in private employment did not violate the 1964 Civil Rights Act. The Court's majority pointed out the difference between this case and the *Bakke* case. Public institutions receiving federal funds could not discriminate on the basis of race. Private employers, however, could use quotas in programs aimed at ending racial injustice.

★ The Court Ruled on the Right to Privacy

Can a state make it a crime for a woman to end her pregnancy? The right to have an abortion is part of a larger issue: the right of privacy.

Roe v. Wade. In 1973, Supreme Court Justice Harry A. Blackmun wrote: "The Constitution does not explicitly mention any right of privacy." Yet Blackmun went on to say that in many cases the Court had recognized such a right.

Blackmun's support of the right of privacy appeared in the opinion he wrote for the 7-to-2 majority in *Roe* v. *Wade*. This key

reverse discrimination *treating a group of people unfairly in an attempt to help another group already treated unfairly*

quota a specified number or proportion used in affirmative action programs

In 1978 the Supreme Court ruled that Allan Bakke was the victim of reverse discrimination and ordered his admission to the medical school at the University of California at Davis. Nevertheless, the Court approved affirmative action programs based on race that did not involve the use of rigid quotas.

decision struck down a Texas law that banned nearly all abortions. While saying that women had the right to end a pregnancy, the Court also declared that there were limits to this right. A state could still prevent women from having abortions during the final three months of pregnancy in order to protect the life of the unborn child.

In several cases since *Roe,* the Court has made it more possible for state legislatures to adopt stricter regulation of abortion. In two 1990 cases, the Court ruled that a state may require a minor to inform at least one parent before she can obtain an abortion (*Ohio* v. *Akron Center for Reproductive Health*) and to tell both parents of her plans, except in cases where a judge gives permission for an abortion without parental knowledge (*Minnesota* v. *Hodgson*).

In 1992, the Court ruled, in *Planned Parenthood of Southeastern Pennsylvania* v. *Casey*, that a state may place reasonable limits on a women's right to choose an abortion. Those restrictions, however, cannot impose an "undue burden" on her choice of that procedure.

★ Should The Court Be a Policy Maker?

Through most of its history, the Supreme Court has not played an important role in making government policy. Using its power of judicial review cautiously, it has limited itself to striking down federal and state laws that it viewed as clearly unconstitutional. Thus, rather than making laws, the Court has generally reviewed existing laws passed by states and the federal government.

During much of the last three decades, though, the Court has taken a more active role in shaping public policy. The Court has often taken the lead in addressing the nation's social and political problems, ruling on constitutional questions whenever possible. This approach is referred to as *judicial activism*. Those who favor a Supreme Court that rules on many issues of public policy are known as judicial activists. Often judicial activists are politically liberal.

judicial activism a philosophy that maintains the Supreme Court should rule on constitutional questions and issues of public policy as often as possible

judicial restraint a philosophy that maintains the Supreme Court should not make public policy and should take action only when the Constitution is clearly violated

Those who object to an active role for the Supreme Court favor a policy of *judicial restraint*. This group, generally people who dislike the Court's liberal decisions on social issues, want the Supreme Court to let the legislative and executive branches of government make public-policy decisions. A Supreme Court guided by judicial restraint would take action only when the Constitution was violated in some clear and specific way. In 1987, this issue of judicial activism versus judicial restraint received considerable public attention. President Reagan nominated Robert Bork to fill a vacancy on the Supreme Court. Bork favored judicial restraint. The U.S. Senate conducted confirmation hearings, applying its constitutional power to review a President's nominee to the High Court. The Senate voted 58-42 against Bork, largely on the grounds that his judicial philosophy was too strongly in favor of judicial restraint.

Like the other recurring issues, the question of judicial activism versus judicial restraint is one that has never been entirely resolved and probably will never completely disappear.

Section 5 Review

1. **Defining Constitutional Terms**

   Write a brief definition for each of the following terms.

   a. capital punishment _____

   b. affirmative action _____

   c. reverse discrimination _____

   d. quota _____

   e. judicial activism _____

   f. judicial restraint _____

2. **Reviewing Social Studies Skills:** Recognizing Point of View

   Circle the Supreme Court decisions that a supporter of judicial restraint would probably disapprove of.

   School District of Abington Township v. *Schempp*
   Furman v. *Georgia*
   Proffitt v. *Florida*
   Regents of University of California v. *Bakke*
   Roe v. *Wade*

3. **Reviewing the Main Ideas**

   Write a brief answer — one or two sentences — for each of the following questions.

   a. On what grounds has the Supreme Court ruled against laws allowing prayer in public schools? _____

   _____

   b. Why did the Supreme Court change its ruling on the death penalty? _____

   _____

   c. In the Court's view, when are racial quotas considered a form of reverse discrimination?

   _____

   _____

   d. In what ways has the Supreme Court limited a woman's right to an abortion? _____

   _____

   _____

   e. How is the philosophy of judicial activism different from the philosophy of judicial restraint?

   _____

   _____

4. **Critical Thinking Skills:** Understanding the Constitution

   On a separate sheet of paper, answer the following question in a brief paragraph.

   What trend, or tendency, can you detect in the Supreme Court's decisions on school prayer cases beginning with *Engel* v. *Vitale* (1962)?

Hazelwood School District v. Kuhlmeier

It is Monday morning. You arrive at school a little early and run down to the office where the school newspaper is prepared. The latest edition of the weekly paper is hot off the presses, and you are eager to see how it came out. You are especially excited because the first article you ever wrote is to be featured on page one. When you arrive at the office you discover that half of the first page, including the space where your article was to appear, is blacked out.

You immediately assume that the printers made a mistake. But your fellow reporters inform you that the school's principal purposefully blacked out two front-page stories because he thought they were too controversial. Is this fair? More important, is it legal?

Are students protected by the First Amendment right to free expression? In October 1987, the U.S. Supreme Court heard arguments in a case that decided whether student reporters are protected by the same First Amendment rights as are adult reporters. The case, *Hazelwood School District et al v. Kuhlmeier et al,* involved the principal and three student reporters from Hazelwood East High School, in Hazelwood, Missouri.

A Special Edition of the *Spectrum*

In 1983, Cathy Kuhlmeier, Leslie Smart, and Leanne Tippet were reporters for the *Spectrum,* Hazelwood East's weekly student newspaper. In May of that year the three students devoted a two-page special section of the *Spectrum* to articles on problems facing high-school students. Issues such as parental divorce, teenage pregnancy, and runaway teens were featured.

Dr. Reynolds Responds

The *Spectrum* already had a reputation for publishing controversial articles, and Hazelwood's principal, Dr. Robert Reynolds, kept a close watch on the kinds of articles students were writing. When Dr. Reynolds read early versions of some of the articles scheduled for the May issue, he decided they were too controversial.

One story was about a student whose family was going through a painful divorce. The reporter interviewed a student who explained her views of the

Are students protected by the First Amendment right to free expression? That's the question Attorney Leslie Edwards (left) and students Leslie Smart (center) and Leanne Tippett raised.

causes of her parents' problems. Although the reporter had removed the student's name from the final version of the story, her name appeared in the earlier version that the principal read. Dr. Reynolds felt that the story was an invasion of the student's and her family's privacy. Dr. Reynolds also objected to a story about three pregnant Hazelwood students. He thought that the story presented teenage pregnancy in a positive light and, therefore, would not permit its publication. The students working on the newspaper had written other articles for the special section discussing the difficulties of teen pregnancy. One article discussed the high failure rate of teenage marriages. Still, Dr. Reynolds felt that the material was inappropriate. He decided that the entire two-page supplement should not be published. Thus, when the May issue of *Spectrum* came out, none of the articles on teenage problems appeared.

The Students Respond

Believing that their First Amendment rights of free speech and press had been violated, the three reporters — Kuhlmeier, Smart, and Lippett — filed a lawsuit in 1983 against their principal. They claimed that the *Spectrum* was a public forum — a place where people could express their views freely.

The first court to hear the case, the U.S. District Court in St. Louis, ruled in 1985 that the principal and the school had a right to control what was published in the school newspaper. The court explained that the *Spectrum* was part of the school curriculum and that journalism students received course credit for their work. The principal, then, was exercising his responsibility for the students' education.

Employing their constitutional right to appeal a court's verdict, the student reporters asked the U.S. Court of Appeals in 1985 to reconsider the case. In July 1986, the Court of Appeals overturned the lower district court ruling. Two of the three justices agreed with the students that the *Spectrum* was a public forum. As such, the student newspaper was protected by the First Amendment.

The Hazelwood School District then appealed the case to the U.S. Supreme Court. On October 13, 1987, the Supreme Court heard arguments from both sides in the dispute.

Arguments for the School District

1. The school district had the right to control a student newspaper published with the public's money if the school had a stated policy to do so.
2. The district should have broad control over the newspaper's content because it was part of the journalism curriculum. Students wrote articles for academic credit in a course.

Arguments for the Student Reporters

1. The *Spectrum* is a public forum, and as such is protected by the First Amendment right to freedom of expression.
2. Public school officials should not be able to censor school-financed newspapers simply because they disagree with the paper's viewpoint.

In January 1988, the Supreme Court issued a ruling in this case. What are the constitutional and legal issues raised by this case? Suppose you were writing the Court's opinion. In whose favor would you decide? The school district's or the student reporters'? Write your Supreme Court decision in the space below, keeping in mind the issues you have identified.

_____

_____

_____

_____

_____

_____

_____

_____

5 The Annotated Constitution

"What have you created here?"

"A republic, if we can keep it."

—Ben Franklin

The Preamble of the Constitution begins with the famous words, "We the people of the United States . . ." These words immediately point up a major difference between the Constitution and the Articles of Confederation. The Articles, with their emphasis on states' rights, begin "We the states. . . " Under the Articles, then, ruling power came from the states. Under the Constitution, all power comes from the people.

The United States was the first nation to base its system of government on a single document. Two hundred years later, the Constitution remains the basic law of the land. It is now the oldest written constitution still in force at a national level. Not surprisingly, many other countries have used the U.S. Constitution as a model of how to create a lasting and stable system of government.

Why has the Constitution continued to be vital and relevant for more than two centuries? Probably because the Framers used it to create the *framework* of a government. By concentrating on general principles and basic freedoms, the delegates who gathered in Philadelphia ensured that the Constitution would not become dated or unworkable after a few decades. By contrast, state constitutions are often 10 times longer and full of small details. Most of these state constitutions have had to be thoroughly updated or replaced on more than one occasion.

A complete copy of the U.S. Constitution is reproduced in this chapter. To help you understand it better, easier-to-read paraphrases are included in the margins. Additional information also appears in the margin and is printed in italics. The parts of the Constitution that have been changed by amendment or are no longer in effect have been crossed out. In addition, spelling and punctuation have been updated, and a short introduction has been included before each main part of the document.

On the final day of the Constitutional Convention, someone asked Benjamin Franklin, "What have you created here?" Franklin answered, "A republic, if we can keep it." Studying the Constitution is one of the best ways to learn more about that republic and how it works.

The Constitution of the United States of America

Preamble

We the people of the United States, in order to form a more perfect union, establish justice, insure domestic tranquility, provide for the common defense, promote the general welfare, and secure the blessings of liberty to ourselves and our posterity, do ordain and establish this Constitution for the United States of America.

The Preamble sets the tone of the Constitution and states its goals. It explains that the Constitution was written to guarantee peace and liberty for all United States citizens and their descendants.

The Preamble was written last, after all other parts of the Constitution were decided.

Introduction to Article I

Article I outlines the legislative or lawmaking branch of the government, made up of the House of Representatives and the Senate. The ten sections of this Article describe the day-by-day operations of Congress— such as qualifications for membership, the electing process, and the process by which a bill becomes a law—as well as the powers Congress has as one of the three branches of government.

Article I   Legislative Branch

Section I   Congress in general

All legislative powers herein granted shall be vested in a Congress of the United States, which shall consist of a Senate and House of Representatives.

The power to make laws is given to the Senate and the House of Representatives.

Section 2   The House of Representatives

1. The House of Representatives shall be composed of members chosen every second year by the people of the several states, and the electors in each state shall have the qualifications requisite for electors of the most numerous branch of the state legislature.

House members are elected every two years by people qualified to vote for members of the largest house of their state legislature.

2. No person shall be a representative who shall not have attained to the age of twenty-five years, and been seven years a citizen of the United States, and who shall not, when elected, be an inhabitant of that state in which he shall be chosen.

House members must be at least twenty-five years old, U.S. citizens for seven years, and residents of the states that elect them.

3. Representatives and direct taxes shall be apportioned among the several states which may be included within this Union, according to their respective numbers, [which shall be determined by adding to the

The number of representatives allowed each state depends on the state's population.

This is known as the "three-fifths compromise," which settled the problem of how slaves were to be counted.

The population of the states shall be determined by a federal census taken every ten years.

The first census was taken in 1790.

The governor of the state calls special elections to fill vacancies in that state's representation.

The House chooses its own officers. It alone has the power to accuse a government official of a crime.

Each state is allowed two senators.

Senators are now elected directly.

Senate elections are arranged so that one third of the senators are elected every two years for six-year terms.

Originally vacancies in the Senate were filled by the state legislature. This process was changed by Amendment 17.

Senators must be at least thirty years old, United States citizens for at least nine years, and residents of the states that elect them.

The Vice-President is president of the Senate but only votes in ties.

whole number of free persons, including those bound to service for a term of years, and excluding Indians not taxed, three fifths of all other persons]. The actual enumeration shall be made within three years after the first meeting of the Congress of the United States, and within every subsequent term of ten years, in such manner as they shall by law direct. The number of representatives shall not exceed one for every thirty thousand, but each state shall have at least one representative; [and until such enumeration shall be made, the state of New Hampshire shall be entitled to choose 3, Massachusetts 8, Rhode Island and Providence Plantations 1, Connecticut 5, New York 6, New Jersey 4, Pennsylvania 8, Delaware 1, Maryland 6, Virginia 10, North Carolina 5, South Carolina 5, and Georgia 3].

4. When vacancies happen in the representation from any state, the executive authority thereof shall issue writs of election to fill such vacancies.

5. The House of Representatives shall choose their speaker and other officers; and shall have the sole power of impeachment.

Section 3 The Senate

1. The Senate of the United States shall be composed of two senators from each state, chosen [by the legislature thereof,] for six years; and each senator shall have one vote.

2. Immediately after they shall be assembled in consequence of the first election, they shall be divided as equally as may be into three classes. [The seats of the senators of the first class shall be vacated at the expiration of the second year, of the second class at the expiration of the fourth year, and of the third class at the expiration of the sixth year,] so that one third may be chosen every second year; [and if vacancies happen by resignation, or otherwise, during the recess of the legislature of any state, the executive thereof may make temporary appointments until the next meeting of the legislature, which shall then fill such vacancies.]

3. No person shall be a senator who shall not have attained to the age of thirty years, and been nine years a citizen of the United States, and who shall not, when elected, be an inhabitant of that state for which he shall be chosen.

4. The Vice-President of the United States shall be president of the Senate, but shall have no vote, unless they be equally divided.

5. The Senate shall choose their other officers, and also a president pro tempore, in the absence of the Vice-President, or when he shall exercise the office of President of the United States.

6. The Senate shall have the sole power to try all impeachments. When sitting for that purpose, they shall be on oath or affirmation. When the President of the United States is tried, the chief justic shall preside; and no person shall be convicted without the concurrence of two thirds of the members present.

7. Judgment in cases of impeachment shall not extend further than to removal from office, and disqualification to hold and enjoy any office of honor, trust, or profit under the United States; but the party convicted shall, nevertheless, be liable and subject to indictment, trial, judgment, and punishment, according to law.

Section 4 The electoral process

1. The times, places, and manner of holding elections for senators and representatives shall be prescribed in each state by the legislature thereof; but the Congress may at any time by law make or alter such regulations, except as to the places of choosing senators.

2. The Congress shall assemble at least once in every year, [and such meeting shall be on the first Monday in December,] unless they shall by law appoint a different day.

Section 5 Rules of procedure

1. Each House shall be the judge of the elections, returns, and qualifications of its own members, and a majority of each shall constitute a quorum to do business; but a smaller number may adjourn from day to day, and may be authorized to compel the attendance of absent members, in such manner, and under such penalties, as each House may provide.

2. Each House may determine the rules of its proceedings, punish its members from disorderly behavior, and, with the concurrence of two thirds, expel a member.

3. Each House shall keep a journal of its proceedings, and from time to time publish the same, excepting such parts as may in their judgment require secrecy; and the yeas and nays of the members of either House on any question shall, at the desire of one fifth of those present, be entered on the journal.

The Senate elects its own officers, including a temporary president if needed.

The Senate tries all impeachment cases. A two-thirds vote is necessary for conviction.

The Senate can remove from office those officials it convicts on impeachment charges, but any further punishment must come by way of trial in regular courts of law.

Election regulations are left to the states, though Congress may pass certain laws concerning elections.

Congress must meet at least once a year.
Amendment 20 sets January 3 as the date for a session to begin.

Each house of Congress has the right to judge the elections and qualifications of its members. To conduct official business, each house must have a majority of its members present.

Each house may make rules for its members. Members may be expelled by a two-thirds vote.

Each house of Congress must keep a journal and publish a record of its activities.

Neither house may adjourn for more than three days without the permission of the other house.

Members of Congress are paid a salary. With certain exceptions, members cannot be sued or arrested for anything they say in Congress.

Members of Congress may not hold any other federal office while serving in Congress.

All money bills must begin in the House. The Senate may amend such bills.

A bill passed by both houses of Congress goes to the President. If the President approves the bill, it becomes a law. If the President vetoes a bill, it goes back to Congress. Congress may pass a bill into law over the President's veto by a two-thirds vote.

The veto and the override are examples of the checks and balances built into the federal government. In 1947 the Taft-Hartley Act was passed over President Truman's veto.
A bill becomes a law if the President holds it unsigned for ten days, unless Congress adjourns.

4. Neither House, during the session of Congress, shall, without the consent of the other, adjourn for more than three days, nor to any other place than that in which the two Houses shall be sitting.

Section 6 Compensation, privileges, and restrictions

1. The senators and representatives shall receive a compensation for their services, to be ascertained by law, and paid out of the Treasury of the United States. They shall in all cases, except treason, felony, and breach of the peace, be privileged from arrest during their attendance at the session of their respective houses, and in going to and returning from the same; and for any speech or debate in either house, they shall not be questioned in any other place.

2. No senator or representative shall, during the time for which he was elected, be appointed to any civil office under the authority of the United States, which shall have been created, or the emoluments whereof shall have been increased during such time; and no person holding any office under the United States shall be a member of either house during his continuance in office.

Section 7 Method of passing laws

1. All bills for raising revenue shall originate in the House of Representatives; but the Senate may propose or concur with amendments as on other bills.

2. Every bill which shall have passed the House of Representatives and the Senate shall, before it becomes a law, be presented to the President of the United States; if he approves he shall sign it, but if not he shall return it with his objections to that house in which it shall have originated, who shall enter the objections at large on their journal, and proceed to reconsider it. If after such reconsideration two thirds of that house shall agree to pass the bill, it shall be sent, together with the objections, to the other house, by which it shall likewise be reconsidered, and if approved by two thirds of that house, it shall become a law. But in all such cases the votes of both houses shall be determined by yeas and nays, and the names of the persons voting for and against the bill shall be entered on the journal of each house respectively. If any bill shall not be returned by the President within ten days (Sundays excepted) after it shall have been presented to him, the same shall be a law, in like manner as if he had signed it, unless the Congress by their adjournment prevent its return, in which case it shall not be a law.

3. Every order, resolution, or vote to which the concurrence of the Senate and House of Representatives may be necessary (except on a question of adjournment) shall be presented to the President of the United States; and before the same shall take effect, shall be approved by him, or being disapproved by him, shall be repassed by two thirds of the Senate and House of Representatives, according to the rules and limitations prescribed in the case of a bill.

Every order or resolution of Congress should be presented to the President.

Actually, many congressional resolutions do not go to the President. But any bill that is to become a law must be sent to the President.

Section 8 Powers granted to Congress

The Congress shall have power:

1. To lay and collect taxes, duties, imposts, and excises, to pay the debts and provide for the common defense and general welfare of the United States; but all duties, imposts, and excises shall be uniform throughout the United States;

CONGRESS HAS THE POWER TO:
collect taxes and pay debts; provide for the defense and welfare of the United States;

2. To borrow money on the credit of the United States;

borrow money;

3. To regulate commerce with foreign nations, and among the several states, and with the Indian tribes;

regulate trade;

4. To establish a uniform rule of naturalization, and uniform laws on the subject of bankruptcies throughout the United States;

establish uniform laws concerning citizenship and bankruptcy;

5. To coin money, regulate the value thereof, and of foreign coin, and fix the standard of weights and measures;

coin money and fix standards of weights and measures;

6. To provide for the punishment of counterfeiting the securities and current coin of the United States;

fix punishment for counterfeiting money;

7. To establish post offices and post roads;

establish post offices and roads;

8. To promote the progress of science and useful arts by securing for limited times to authors and inventors the exclusive right to their respective writings and discoveries;

issue patents and copyrights;

9. To constitute tribunals inferior to the Supreme Court;

set up federal courts;

10. To define and punish piracies and felonies committed on the high seas, and offenses against the law of nations;

punish piracies;

11. To declare war, [grant letters of marque and reprisal,] and make rules concerning captures on land and water;

declare war; raise and support armies;

maintain a navy;

make regulations for the armed forces;

provide, in case of emergency, for calling out the national guard;

maintain and train the national guard;

make laws for the District of Columbia and other federal properties;

To win southern support for his economic plan in 1790, Hamilton supported a southern city, Washington, D.C., as the capital.

make all laws "necessary and proper." *This is the "elastic clause," which allows Congress to make laws not specifically mentioned in the Constitution.*

CONGRESS MAY NOT:

This clause, referring to the slave trade until 1808, has no effect today.

illegally imprison people;

pass laws of unfair punishment;

pass any direct tax unless it is in proportion to population (except the income tax, which is allowed by Amendment 16); tax exports;

12. To raise and support armies; but no appropriation of money to that use shall be for a longer term than two years;

13. To provide and maintain a navy;

14. To make rules for the government and regulation of the land and naval forces;

15. To provide for calling forth the militia to execute the laws of the union, suppress insurrections, and repel invasions;

16. To provide for organizing, arming, and disciplining the militia, and for governing such part of them as may be employed in the service of the United States, reserving to the states respectively the appointment of the officers and the authority of training the militia according to the discipline prescribed by Congress;

17. To exercise exclusive legislation in all cases whatsoever over such district—not exceeding ten miles square—as may, by cession of particular states, and the acceptance of Congress, become the seat of the government of the United States, and to exercise like authority over all places purchased by the consent of the legislature of the state in which the same shall be for the erection of forts, magazines, arsenals, dockyards, and other needful buildings; and

18. To make all laws which shall be necessary and proper for carrying into execution the foregoing powers and all other powers vested by this Constitution in the government of the United States, or in any department or officer thereof.

Section 9 Powers denied to the federal government

1. [The migration or importation of such persons as any of the states now existing shall think proper to admit shall not be prohibited by the Congress prior to the year one thousand eight hundred and eight, but a tax or duty may be imposed on such importation, not exceeding ten dollars for each person.]

2. The privilege of the writ of *habeas corpus* shall not be suspended, unless when in cases of rebellion or invasion the public safety may require it.

3. No bill of attainder or *ex post facto* law shall be passed.

4. No capitation or other direct tax shall be laid, unless in proportion to the census or enumeration herein before directed to be taken.

5. No tax or duty shall be laid on articles exported from any state.

6. No preference shall be given by any regulation of commerce or revenue to the ports of one state over those of another; nor shall vessels bound to or from one state be obliged to enter, clear, or pay duties in another.

7. No money shall be drawn from the Treasury, but in consequence of appropriations made by law; and a regular statement and account of the receipts and expenditures of all public money shall be published from time to time.

8. No title of nobility shall be granted by the United States; and no person holding any office of profit or trust under them shall, without the consent of the Congress, accept of any present, emolument, office, or title of any kind whatever from any king, prince, or foreign state.

Section 10 Powers denied to the states

1. No state shall enter into any treaty, alliance, or confederation; grant letters of marque and reprisal; coin money; emit bills of credit; make anything but gold and silver coin a tender in payment of debts; pass any bill of attainder, *ex post facto* law, or law impairing the obligation of contracts, or grant any title of nobility.

2. No state shall, without the consent of Congress, lay any imposts or duties on imports or exports, except what may be absolutely necessary for executing its inspection laws; and the net produce of all duties and imposts laid by any state on imports or exports shall be for the use of the Treasury of the United States; and all such laws shall be subject to the revision and control of the Congress.

3. No state shall, without the consent of Congress, lay any duty of tonnage, keep troops, or ships of war in time of peace, enter into any agreement or compact with another state, or with a foreign power, or engage in war, unless actually invaded, or in such imminent danger as will not admit of delay.

pass any law that would favor the trade of a particular state;

spend money that has not been authorized by law;

grant any title of nobility. No government officials may accept gifts or titles from other nations unless Congress approves.

STATE GOVERNMENTS MAY NOT:

make treaties or alliances; coin money; give bills of credit; grant titles of nobility;

tax imports or exports without the consent of Congress;
This section spells out the powers denied to the states in an attempt to avoid disputes like those that arose under the Articles of Confederation.

tax ships without the consent of Congress; keep a regular army; make agreements with other states or with foreign countries; or engage in war, unless invaded or in grave danger.

Article II, which describes the executive branch, was the most hotly debated part of the Constitution. Experience during colonial times had shown many executives—the king and his governors in the colonies—to be tyrants. So the writers of the Constitution were careful to provide many checks on the President's power. Article II outlines the President's term of office, method of election, qualifications, powers, and duties. It also provides a way for removing a President from office if that President commits a high crime.

Article II Executive Branch

Section I President and Vice-President

1. The executive power shall be vested in a President of the United States of America. He shall hold his office during the term of four years, and together with the Vice-President, chosen for the same term, be elected as follows:

2. Each state shall appoint, in such manner as the legislature thereof may direct, a number of electors equal to the whole number of senators and representatives to which the state may be entitled in the Congress; but no senator or representative, or person holding an office of trust or profit under the United States, shall be appointed an elector.

3. The electors shall meet in their respective states, and vote by ballot for two persons, of whom one at least shall not be an inhabitant of the same state with themselves. And they shall make a list of all persons voted for, and of the number of votes for each; which list they shall sign and certify, and transmit sealed to the seat of the government of the United States, directed to the president of the Senate. The president of the Senate shall, in the presence of the Senate and House of Representatives, open all the certificates, and the votes shall then be counted. The person having the greatest number of votes shall be the President, if such number be a majority of the whole number of electors appointed; and if there be more than one who have such a majority, and have an equal number of votes, then the House of Representatives shall immediately choose by ballot one of them for President; and if no person have a majority, then from the five highest on the list the said house shall in like manner choose the President. But in choosing the President, the votes shall be taken by states, the representation from each state having one vote; a quorum for this purpose shall consist of a member or members from two thirds of the states, and a majority of all the states shall be neces-

The executive power is given to the President who holds office for a four-year term.

The President is elected by an electoral college made up of electors appointed by the states. The number of electors given to each state equals the number of its senators and representatives.

This method of electing a President and Vice-President has been changed by Amendment 12.

sary to a choice. In every case, after the choice of the President, the person having the greatest number of votes of the electors shall be the Vice-President. But if there should remain two or more who have equal votes, the Senate shall choose from them by ballot the Vice-President.]

4. The Congress may determine the time of choosing the electors, and the day on which they shall give their votes; which day shall be the same throughout the United States.

Congress determines when electors are chosen and when they will vote.

5. No person except a natural-born citizen [or a citizen of the United States at the time of the adoption of this Constitution,] shall be eligible to the office of President; neither shall any person be eligible to that office who shall not have attained to the age of thirty-five years and been fourteen years a resident within the United States.

The President must be a natural-born citizen of the United States, at least thirty-five years old, and a resident of the United States for at least fourteen years.

6. In case of the removal of the President from office, or of his death, resignation, or inability to discharge the powers and duties of the said office, the same shall devolve on the Vice-President, and the Congress may by law provide for the case of removal, death, resignation, or inability, both of the President and Vice-President, declaring what officer shall then act as President, and such officer shall act accordingly, until the disability be removed, or a President shall be elected.

This section has been modified by Amendment 25.

7. The President shall at stated times receive for his services a compensation, which shall neither be increased nor diminished during the period for which he shall have been elected, and he shall not receive within that period any other emolument from the United States, or any of them.

The President receives a salary, which cannot be lowered or raised during the term in office.

8. Before he enter on the execution of his office, he shall take the following oath or affirmation:—"I do solemnly swear (or affirm) that I will faithfully execute the office of President of the United States, and will to the best of my ability, preserve, protect, and defend the Constitution of the United States."

Before taking office, the President takes this oath, which is usually administered by the chief justice of the Supreme Court.

Section 2 Powers of the President

1. The President shall be commander in chief of the army and navy of the United States, and of the militia of the several states, when called into the actual service of the United States; he may require the opinion in writing of the principal officer in each of the executive departments upon any subject relating to the duties of their respective offices, and he shall have power to grant reprieves and pardons for offenses against the United States, except in cases of impeachment.

The President is commander in chief of the armed forces.

The President can grant delays of punishment and pardons for offenses against the United States, except in impeachment cases.

103

The President has the power to make treaties and to appoint ambassadors and other officers. The Senate must approve such appointments. Minor appointments may be made without Senate approval.

The right of the Senate to approve appointments was new with the Constitution.

When the Senate is not in session, the President may make temporary appointments to office.

The President is required to report to Congress on the state of the Union, to receive ambassadors, to see that all laws are executed, and to commission all officers of the United States. He also has the power to call special sessions of Congress.

The President and all other civil officers of the United States may be removed from office if convicted of treason, bribery, or other high crimes.

2. He shall have power, by and with the advice and consent of the Senate, to make treaties, provided two thirds of the senators present concur; and he shall nominate and, by and with the advice and consent of the Senate, shall appoint ambassadors, other public ministers and consuls, judges of the Supreme Court, and all other officers of the United States whose appointments are not herein otherwise provided for, and which shall be established by law; but the Congress may by law vest the appointment of such inferior officers as they think proper in the President alone, in the courts of law, or in the heads of departments.

3. The President shall have power to fill up all vacancies that may happen during the recess of the Senate, by granting commissions which shall expire at the end of their next session.

Section 3 Duties of the President

He shall from time to time give to the Congress information of the state of the Union, and recommend to their consideration such measures as he shall judge necessary and expedient; he may, on extraordinary occasions, convene both houses, or either of them, and in case of disagreement between them with respect to the time of adjournment, he may adjourn them to such time as he shall think proper; he shall receive ambassadors and other public ministers; he shall take care that the laws be faithfully executed, and shall commission all the officers of the United States.

Section 4 Impeachment

The President, Vice-President, and all civil officers of the United States shall be removed from office on impeachment for, and conviction of, treason, bribery, or other high crimes and misdemeanors.

Introduction to Article III

Article III outlines the last of the three branches of government — the judicial branch. By creating a court system, the writers of the Constitution found a way for the government to enforce its laws and settle disputes peacefully. Besides describing the federal court system, Article III defines the crime and punishment of treason.

Article III Judicial Branch

Section 1 The federal courts

The judicial power of the United States shall be vested in one Supreme Court, and in such inferior courts as the Congress may from time to time ordain and establish. The judges, both of the Supreme and inferior courts, shall hold their offices during good behavior and shall at stated times receive for their services a compensation, which shall not be diminished during their continuance in office.

Judicial power is given to a Supreme Court and other lesser courts authorized by Congress. Federal judges can hold office for life if they are not impeached and convicted for committing crimes.

Section 2 Jurisdiction of the federal courts

1. The judicial power shall extend to all cases in law and equity arising under this Constitution, the laws of the United States, and treaties made, or which shall be made, under their authority; to all cases affecting ambassadors, other public ministers and consuls; to all cases of admiralty and maritime jurisdiction; to controversies to which the United States shall be a party; to controversies between two or more states; [between a state and citizens of another state;] between citizens of different states; between citizens of the same state claiming lands under grants of different states, and between a state, or the citizens thereof, and foreign states, citizens, or subjects.

The federal courts try all cases involving the Constitution, federal laws, and treaties. Lawsuits involving the federal government, two states, or citizens of different states are tried in federal courts.

Amendment 11 changes this part. The case of Cherokee Nation v. Georgia *in 1831 rested on this part of the Constitution.*

2. In all cases affecting ambassadors, other public ministers and consuls, and those in which a state shall be a party, the Supreme Court shall have original jurisdiction. In all the other cases before mentioned, the Supreme Court shall have appellate jurisdiction, both as to law and fact, with such exceptions, and under such regulations as the Congress shall make.

Cases involving ambassadors or officials of foreign nations or those involving states are tried in the Supreme Court. Other cases begin in lesser courts but may be appealed to the Supreme Court.

3. The trial of all crimes, except in cases of impeachment, shall be by jury; and such trial shall be held in the state where the said crimes shall have been committed; but when not committed within any state, the trial shall be at such place or places as the Congress may by law have directed.

All crimes, except in cases of impeachment, shall be tried by jury.

Section 3 Treason

It is an act of treason to wage war against the United States or to give aid to its enemies.

1. Treason against the United States shall consist only in levying war against them, or in adhering to their enemies, giving them aid and comfort. No person shall be convicted of treason, unless on the testimony of two witnesses to the same overt act or on confession in open court.

Congress may fix the punishment for treason, but it may not punish the families of those found guilty of treason.

2. The Congress shall have power to declare the punishment of treason, but no attainder of treason shall work corruption of blood, or forfeiture except during the life of the person attained.

Introduction to Article IV
Article IV describes the relation of the states to one another, new states and territories, and the rights of states that the federal government guarantees.

Article IV The States and the Federal Government

Section 1 State records

The official acts of one state must be recognized as legal by all other states.

Full faith and credit shall be given in each state to the public acts, records, and judicial proceedings of every other state. And the Congress may by general laws prescribe the manner in which such acts, records, and proceedings shall be proved, and the effect thereof.

Section 2 Privileges and immunities of citizens

States must treat citizens of another state as fairly as their own citizens.

1. The citizens of each state shall be entitled to all privileges and immunities of citizens in the several states.

A state governor may demand the return of a criminal who has fled to another state.

2. A person charged in any state with treason, felony, or other crime, who shall flee from justice and be found in another state, shall, on demand of the executive authority of the state from which he fled, be delivered up to be removed to the state, having jurisdiction of the crime.

This provision for the return of runaway slaves has had no effect since Amendment 13 was adopted in 1865.

3. [No person held to service or labor in one state, under the laws thereof, escaping into another shall, in consequence of any law or regulation therein, be discharged from such service or labor, but shall be delivered up on claim of the party to whom such service or labor may be due.]

Section 3 New states and territories

1. New states may be admitted by the Congress into this Union; but no new state shall be formed or erected within the jurisdiction of any other state; nor any state be formed by the junction of two or more states, or parts of states, without the consent of the legislatures of the states concerned, as well as of the Congress.

2. The Congress shall have power to dispose of and make all needful rules and regulations respecting the territory or other property belonging to the United States; and nothing in this Constitution shall be so construed as to prejudice any claims of the United States, or of any particular state.

Section 4 Guarantees to the states

The United States shall guarantee to every state in this union a republican form of government, and shall protect each of them against invasion; and on application of the legislature, or of the executive—when the legislature cannot be convened—against domestic violence.

Introduction to Article V

Article V describes the amending process, the means by which the Constitution can be changed to meet the needs of a changing and growing nation.

Article V Method of Amendment

The Congress, whenever two thirds of both houses shall deem it necessary, shall propose amendments to this Constitution or, on the application of the legislatures of two thirds of the several states, shall call a convention for proposing amendments, which in either case shall be valid to all intents and purposes as part of this Constitution when ratified by the legislatures of three fourths of the several states, or by conventions in three fourths thereof, as the one or the other mode of ratification may be proposed by the Congress; provided that [no amendment which may be made prior to the year one thousand eight hundred and eight shall in any manner affect the first and fourth clauses in the ninth section of the first article, and that no state, without its consent, shall be deprived of its equal suffrage in the Senate.

New states may be admitted into the Union by Congress.

Congress has the power to make rules and regulations for territories and federal property.

The federal government guarantees to each state a republican form of government, protection against invasion, and protection against disturbances within the state.

Amendments to the Constitution may be proposed by either two thirds of both houses of Congress or by two thirds of the states. Amendments may be ratified by either the legislatures of three fourths of the states or by conventions in three fourths of the states.

This clause has not been in effect since 1808.

All money previously borrowed by the confederation government will be repaid under the Constitution.

The Constitution, federal laws, and the treaties of the United States are the supreme law of the land.

All federal and state officials must take an oath of office promising to support the Constitution. There can be no religious requirement for holding office.

This clause shows the separation between church and state in the United States.

The Constitution will take effect when it is approved by nine states. *The Constitution went into effect on March 4, 1789.*

Introduction to Article VI

Article VI includes a clause that allows all the other parts of the Constitution to work. It declares that the Constitution is "the supreme law of the land." As such, it overrides local or state laws that may be in conflict with it.

Article VI General Provisions

1. All debts contracted and engagements entered into before the adoption of this Constitution shall be as valid against the United States under this Constitution as under the Confederation.

2. This Constitution, and the laws of the United States which shall be made in pursuance thereof; and all treaties made, or which shall be made, under the authority of the United States, shall be the supreme law of the land; and the judges in every state shall be bound thereby, anything in the constitution or laws of any state to the contrary notwithstanding.

3. The senators and representatives before mentioned, and the members of the several state legislatures, and all executive and judicial officers, both of the United States and of the several states, shall be bound by oath or affirmation, to support this Constitution; but no religious test shall ever be required as a qualification to any office or public trust under the United States.

Introduction to Article VII

This brief article explains the approval needed before the Constitution can take effect.

Article VII Ratification of the Constitution

The ratification of the conventions of nine states shall be sufficient for the establishment of this Constitution between the states so ratifying the same.

**Amendments to the
Constitution**

The first ten amendments are
known as the Bill of Rights.
The dates on which these and

the other amendments were
declared ratified are shown in
parentheses.

Amendment 1 (1791)

Congress shall make no law respecting an establishment of religion, or prohibiting the free exercise thereof; or abridging the freedom of speech, or of the press; or the right of the people peaceably to assemble, and to petition the government for a redress of grievances.

The Congress may not make laws interfering with the freedoms of religion, speech, the press, assembly, and petition.

Amendment 2 (1791)

A well-regulated militia being necessary to the security of a free state, the right of the people to keep and bear arms shall not be infringed.

The states have the right to maintain national guard units.

Amendment 3 (1791)

No soldier shall, in time of peace, be quartered in any house without the consent of the owner, nor in time of war, but in a manner to be prescribed by law.

Troops cannot be lodged in private homes during peacetime.

Amendment 4 (1791)

The right of the people to be secure in their persons, houses, papers, and effects against unreasonable searches and seizures shall not be violated, and no warrants shall issue but upon probable cause, supported by oath or affirmation, and particularly describing the place to be searched and the persons or things to be seized.

People are protected against unreasonable searches and arrests.

Amendments 3 and 4 grew out of colonial grievances against the acts of British Parliament.

Amendment 5 (1791)

No person shall be held to answer for a capital or otherwise infamous crime, unless on a presentment or indictment of a grand jury, except in cases arising in the land or naval forces, or in the militia, when in actual service in time of war or public danger; nor shall any person be subject for the same offense to be twice put in jeopardy of life or limb; nor shall be compelled in any criminal case to be a witness against himself, nor be deprived of life, liberty, or property without due process of law; nor shall private property be taken for public use without just compensation.

A person cannot be tried for a crime punishable by death unless charged by a grand jury, be tried twice for the same crime, nor be forced to testify against himself or herself. A person may not be deprived of life, liberty, or property except by lawful means. The government must pay a fair price for property taken for public use.

A person accused of a crime has a right to a speedy public trial by jury, information about the accusation, help from the court in bringing favorable witnesses to the trial, and the aid of a lawyer.

Amendments 4, 5, 6 and 8 are sometimes called a "bill of rights" for people accused of a crime.

In civil lawsuits involving more than $20, the right to a jury trial is guaranteed.

Bails, fines, and punishments cannot be unreasonable.

The basic rights of the people cannot be denied, even those not named in the Constitution.

The powers not given to the federal government are to be held by the states or the people.

Federal courts do not have the power to hear suits brought against a state by the citizens of another state or by foreigners.

Amendment 6 (1791)

In all criminal prosecutions the accused shall enjoy the right to a speedy and public trial by an impartial jury of the state and district wherein the crime shall have been committed, which district shall have been previously ascertained by law, and to be informed of the nature and cause of the accusation; to be confronted with the witnesses against him; to have compulsory process for obtaining witnesses in his favor, and to have the assistance of counsel for his defense.

Amendment 7 (1791)

In suits at common law, where the value in controversy shall exceed twenty dollars, the right of trial by jury shall be preserved, and no fact tried by a jury shall be otherwise reexamined in any court of the United States than according to the rules of the common law.

Amendment 8 (1791)

Excessive bail shall not be required, nor excessive fines imposed, nor cruel and unusual punishments inflicted.

Amendment 9 (1791)

The enumeration in the Constitution of certain rights shall not be construed to deny or disparage others retained by the people.

Amendment 10 (1791)

The powers not delegated to the United States by the Constitution, nor prohibited by it to the states, are reserved to the states respectively, or to the people.

Amendment 11 (1798)

The judicial power of the United States shall not be construed to extend to any suit in law or equity, commenced or prosecuted against one of the United States by citizens of another state, or by citizens or subjects of any foreign state.

Amendment 12 (1804)

The electors shall meet in their respective states and vote by ballot for President and Vice-President, one of whom at least shall not be an inhabitant of the same state with themselves; they shall name in their ballots the person voted for as President, and in distinct ballots the person voted for as Vice-President, and they shall make distinct lists of all persons voted for as President, and of all persons voted for as Vice-President, and of the number of votes for each, which lists they shall sign and certify, and transmit sealed to the seat of the government of the United States, directed to the president of the Senate; the president of the senate shall, in the presence of the Senate and House of Representatives, open all the certificates, and the votes shall then be counted; the person having the greatest number of votes for President shall be President, if such number be a majority of the whole number of electors appointed; and if no person have such majority, then from the persons having the highest numbers not exceeding three on the list of those voted for as President the House of Representatives shall choose immediately by ballot the President. But in choosing the President, the votes shall be taken by states, the representation from each state having one vote; a quorum for this purpose shall consist of a member or members from two thirds of the states, and a majority of all the states shall be necessary to a choice. And if the House of Representatives shall not choose a President whenever the right of choice shall devolve upon them, [~~before the fourth day of March next following,~~] then the Vice-President shall act as President, as in the case of the death or other constitutional disability of the President. The person having the greatest number of votes as Vice-President shall be the Vice-President, if such number be a majority of the whole number of electors appointed; and if no person have a majority, then from the two highest numbers on the list the Senate shall choose the Vice-President; a quorum for the purpose shall consist of two thirds of the whole number of senators, and a majority of the whole number shall be necessary to a choice. But no person constitutionally ineligible to the office of President shall be eligible to that of Vice-President of the United States.

The members of the electoral college vote for the President and Vice-President on separate ballots. If no person receives a majority of the electoral votes for President, the House of Representatives elects the President. In such an election the representatives from each state have one vote among them. A majority of these votes is necessary to elect the President.

This amendment was brought about as a result of the election of 1800, when Jefferson and Burr, candidates of the same party, received the same number of votes. Although it was understood that Burr was the candidate for Vice-President, he could have been named President by the House of Representatives.

The reference to March 4 does not apply today, since the President takes office in January. (See Amendment 20.)

If no person receives a majority of the votes for Vice-President, the Senate elects the Vice-President. A majority vote is necessary.

Amendment 13 (1865)

Section 1 Abolition of Slavery

Neither slavery nor involuntary servitude, except as a punishment of crime whereof the party shall have been duly convicted, shall exist within the United States, or any place subject to their jurisdiction.

Slavery is prohibited. Congress is given the power to enforce the abolition of slavery.

Section 2 Enforcement

Congress shall have power to enforce this article by appropriate legislation.

Amendment 14 (1868)

Section 1 Definition of citizenship

All persons born or naturalized in the United States and subject to the jurisdiction thereof are citizens of the United States and of the state wherein they reside. No state shall make or enforce any law which shall abridge the privileges or immunities of citizens of the United States; nor shall any state deprive any person of life, liberty, or property without due process of law; nor deny to any person within its jurisdiction the equal protection of the laws.

Section 2 Apportionment of representatives

Representatives shall be apportioned among the several states according to their respective numbers, counting the whole number of persons in each state [excluding Indians not taxed]. But when the right to vote at any election for the choice of electors for President and Vice-President of the United States, representatives in Congress, the executive and judicial officers of a state, or the members of the legislature thereof, is denied to any of the [male] inhabitants of such state, being [twenty-one years of age and] citizens of the United States, or in any way abridged, except for participation in rebellion or other crime, the basis of representation therein shall be reduced in the proportion which the number of such [male] citizens shall bear to the whole number of [male] citizens [twenty-one years of age] in such state.

Section 3 Disability resulting from insurrection

No person shall be a senator or representative in Congress, or elector of President and Vice-President, or hold any office, civil or military, under the United States, or under any state, who having previously taken an oath as a member of Congress, or as an officer of the United States, or as a member of any state legislature, or as an executive or judicial officer of any state, to support the Constitution of the United States, shall have engaged in insurrection or rebellion against the same, or given aid or comfort to the enemies thereof. But Congress may by a vote of two thirds of each house, remove such disability.

After the Civil War three amendments, numbers 13, 14, and 15, were quickly ratified. The last amendment had passed sixty-one years before.

All people born or naturalized in the United States are citizens. No state may infringe on the rights of citizens of the United States.

This extended the civil rights protection of Amendment 5 to the citizens of individual states.

If a state prevents certain citizens from voting, that state's representation in Congress may be reduced.

This amendment was passed to guarantee newly freed slaves the right to vote. Congress has never applied this penalty.

If a federal officeholder goes against the oath of office and rebels against the country or helps its enemies, that person cannot ever hold a federal office again. Congress may, however, allow such a person to hold office if two thirds of both houses agree.

This section was aimed at keeping former Confederate officials from holding public office after the Civil War.

Section 4 Confederate debt void

The validity of the public debt of the United States, authorized by law, including debts incurred for payments of pensions and bounties for services in suppressing insurrection or rebellion, shall not be questioned. But neither the United States nor any state shall assume or pay any debt or obligation incurred in aid of insurrection or rebellion against the United States, [~~or any claim for the loss or emancipation of any slave~~]; but all such debts, obligations, and claims shall be held illegal and void.

All debts of the Confederate states are declared invalid and may not be paid.

Section 5 Enforcement

The Congress shall have power to enforce, by appropriate legislation, the provisions of this article.

Amendment 15 (1870)

Section 1 The suffrage

The right of citizens of the United States to vote shall not be denied or abridged by the United States or by any state on account of race, color, or previous condition of servitude.

No citizen can be denied the right to vote because of race or color, or because he or she was formerly a slave.

Section 2 Enforcement

The Congress shall have power to enforce this article by appropriate legislation.

Amendment 16 (1913)

The Congress shall have power to lay and collect taxes on incomes, from whatever source derived, without apportionment among the several states, and without regard to any census or enumeration.

Congress has the right to pass an income tax law.

See Article I, Section 9, Clause 4.

Amendment 17 (1913)

1. The Senate of the United States shall be composed of two senators from each state, elected by the people thereof for six years; and each senator shall have one vote. The electors in each state shall have the qualifications requisite for electors of the most numerous branch of the state legislatures.

2. When vacancies happen in the representation of any state in the Senate, the executive authority of such state shall issue writs of election to fill such vacancies, provided that the legislature of any state may empower the executive thereof to make temporary appointments until the people fill the vacancies by election as the legislature may direct.

Senators are to be elected directly by the voters rather than by state legislatures. A vacancy in the Senate is to be filled by a special election called by the governor. The governor may be given power by the state legislature to appoint someone to fill the vacancy until a special election is held.

See Article I, Section 3, first paragraph.

3. [This amendment shall not be so construed as to affect the election or term of any senator chosen before it becomes valid as part of the Constitution.]

Amendment 18 (1919)

Section 1 Prohibition of intoxicating liquors

[After one year from the ratification of this article the manufacture, sale, or transportation of intoxicating liquors within, the importation thereof into, or the exportation thereof from the United States and all territory subject to the jurisdiction thereof for beverage purposes is hereby prohibited.]

Section 2 Enforcement

[The Congress and the several states shall have concurrent power to enforce this article by appropriate legislation.]

Section 3 Limited time for ratification

[This article shall be inoperative unless it shall have been ratified as an amendment to the Constitution by the legislatures of the several states, as provided in the Constitution, within seven years from the date of submission hereof to the states by the Congress.]

Amendment 19 (1920)

The right of citizens of the United States to vote shall not be denied or abridged by the United States or by any state on account of sex.

The Congress shall have power to enforce this article by appropriate legislation.

Amendment 20 (1933)

Section 1 Terms of President, Vice-President, and Congress

The terms of the President and Vice-President shall end at noon on the 20th day of January, and the terms of senators and representatives at noon on the third day of January, of the years in which such terms would have ended if this article had not been ratified; and the terms of their successors shall then begin.

This entire amendment (forbidding the manufacture, sale, or transporting of alcoholic beverages) was repealed by Amendment 21.

Amendments 16–19, all ratified within seven years, grew out of a major period of reform in the nation.

Women have the right to vote.

This amendment was ratified in time for women to vote in the Presidential election of 1920.

The terms of senators and representatives end on January 3 instead of March 4, and the terms of the President and Vice-President end on January 20 rather than March 4.
This is the "lame duck" amendment. By specifying earlier dates for starting new terms of office, this amendment assured that officials who were defeated in an election would not continue to serve (as "lame ducks") for a long time.

Section 2 Sessions of Congress

The Congress shall assemble at least once in every year, and such meeting shall begin at noon on the third day of January, unless they shall by law appoint a different day.

Section 3 Presidential succession

If, at the time fixed for the beginning of the term of the President, the President-elect shall have died, the Vice-President-elect shall become President. If a President shall not have been chosen before the time fixed for the beginning of his term, or if the President-elect shall have failed to qualify, then the Vice-President-elect shall act as President until a President shall have qualified; and the Congress may by law provide for the case wherein neither a President-elect nor a Vice-President-elect shall have qualified, declaring who shall then act as President, or the manner in which one who is to act shall be selected, and such person act accordingly until a President or Vice-President shall have qualified.

If a President-elect dies before taking office, the Vice-President-elect will become President.

If a President-elect is disqualified, the Vice-President-elect will serve as President until the President-elect qualifies. Congress may declare who will serve as President if neither the President-elect nor the Vice-President-elect qualifies.

Section 4 Choice of President by House

The Congress may by law provide for the case of the death of any of the persons from whom the House of Representatives may choose a President whenever the right of choice shall have devolved upon them, and for the case of the death of any of the persons from whom the Senate may choose a Vice-President whenever the right of choice shall have devolved upon them.

A law in effect today provides that the Speaker of the House will serve as President until a President or Vice-President qualifies.

Section 5 Date effective

[Sections 1 and 2 shall take effect on the 15th of October following the ratification of this article.]

Section 6 Limited time for ratification

[This article shall be inoperative unless it shall have been ratified as an amendment to the Constitution by the legislatures of three fourths of the several states within seven years from the date of its submission.]

Amendment 21 (1933)

Section 1 Repeal of Amendment 18

The eighteenth article of amendment to the Constitution of the United States is hereby repealed.

Amendment 18 is repealed.

Section 2 States protected

The transportation or importation into any state, territory, or possession of the United States for delivery or use therein of intoxicating liquors in violation of the laws thereof is hereby prohibited.

Section 3 Limited time for ratification

[This article shall be inoperative unless it shall have been ratified as an amendment to the Constitution by convention in the several states, as provided in the Constitution, within seven years from the date of the submission hereof to the states by the Congress.]

Amendment 22 (1951)

Section 1 Presidential term limited

No person shall be elected to the office of the President more than twice, and no person who has held the office of President, or acted as President, for more than two years of a term to which some other person was elected President shall be elected to the office of the President more than once. [But this article shall not apply to any person holding the office of President when this article was proposed by the Congress, and shall not prevent any person who may be holding the office of President, or acting as President, during the term within which this article becomes operative from holding the office of President or acting as President during the remainder of such term.]

Section 2 Limited time for ratification

[This article shall be inoperative unless it shall have been ratified as an amendment to the Constitution by the legislatures of three fourths of the several states within seven years from the date of its submission to the states by the Congress.]

Amendment 23 (1961)

Section 1 Voting rights of residents of the District of Columbia

The District constituting the seat of government of the United States shall appoint in such manner as the Congress may direct: A number of electors of President and Vice-President equal to the whole number of senators and representatives in Congress to which the district would be entitled if it were a state, but in no event

The President is limited to two terms of office.

Until 1940 no President had served more than two terms in office. This amendment was proposed after Franklin D. Roosevelt won a fourth term as President. Roosevelt died early in his fourth term.

The residents of the District of Columbia are given the right to vote for President and Vice-President.

116

more than the least populous state; they shall be in addition to those appointed by the states, but they shall be considered, for the purposes of the election of President and Vice-President, to be electors appointed by a state; and they shall meet in the district and perform such duties as provided by the twelfth article of amendment.

Section 2 Enforcement

The Congress shall have the power to enforce this article by appropriate legislation.

Amendment 24 (1964)

Section 1 Abolition of poll taxes

The right of citizens of the United States to vote in any primary or other election for President or Vice-President, for electors for President or Vice-President, or for senator or representative in Congress, shall not be denied or abridged by the United States or any state by reason of failure to pay any poll tax or other tax.

No citizen can be made to pay a tax for the right to vote in a federal election.

In 1966 a Supreme Court case found poll taxes on state elections unconstitutional.

Section 2 Enforcement

The Congress shall have the power to enforce this article by appropriate legislation.

Amendment 25 (1967)

Section 1 Presidential succession

In case of the removal of the President from office or his death or resignation, the Vice-President shall become President.

The Vice-President becomes President if the President dies or must leave office.

Section 2 Appointment of new Vice-President

Whenever there is a vacancy in the office of the Vice-President, the President shall nominate a Vice-President who shall take the office upon confirmation by a majority vote of both houses of Congress.

If the office of Vice-President is vacant, the President shall appoint and the Congress approve a new Vice-President.

Section 3 Creation of acting President

Whenever the President transmits to the President pro tempore of the Senate and the Speaker of the House of Representatives his written declaration that he is unable to discharge the powers and duties of his office, and until he transmits to them a written declaration to the contrary, such powers and duties shall be discharged by the Vice-President as acting President.

If the President declares himself unable to continue as President, the Vice-President becomes acting President.

Section 4 Provisions for Presidential disability

Whenever the Vice-President and a majority of either the principal officers of the executive departments, or of such other body as Congress may by law provide, transmit to the president pro tempore of the Senate and the speaker of the House of Representatives their written declaration that the President is unable to discharge the powers and duties of his office, the Vice-President shall immediately assume the powers and duties of the office as acting President.

Thereafter, when the President transmits to the president pro tempore of the Senate and the Speaker of the House of Representatives his written declaration that no inability exists, he shall resume the powers and duties of his office unless the Vice-President and a majority of either the principal officers of the executive department, or of such other body as Congress may by law provide, transmit within four days to the president pro tempore of the Senate and the Speaker of the House of Representatives their written declaration that the President is unable to discharge the powers and duties of his office. Thereupon Congress shall decide the issue, assembling within forty-eight hours for that purpose if not in session. If the Congress, within twenty-one days after receipt of the latter written declaration, or if Congress is not in session, within twenty-one days after Congress is required to assemble, determines by two-thirds vote of both houses that the President is unable to discharge the powers and duties of his office, the Vice-President shall continue to discharge the same as acting President; otherwise, the President shall resume the powers and duties of his office.

Amendment 26 (1971)

Section 1 Voting age lowered

The right of citizens of the United States who are eighteen years of age or older shall not be denied or abridged by the United States or by any state on account of age.

Section 2 Enforcement

The Congress shall have the power to enforce this article by appropriate legislation.

Whenever the Vice-President and a majority of other officers declare that the President is disabled, the Vice-President becomes acting President.

When the President declares that he is again able, he resumes his duties. But if the Vice-President and other officers disagree, Congress decides whether or not the President is able to resume the powers and duties of the office.

Amendment 25 sought a solution to problems that came up on the 1900s when two Presidents — Wilson and Eisenhower — were very sick during their terms. To avoid disputes over who should be in control at such times, this amendment spells out the line of responsibility.

Eighteen-year-olds are given the right to vote.
A Senate report of 1971 concluded that the nation would benefit from the "idealism and concern and energy" of eighteen-year-olds.

Amendment 27 (1992)

No law varying the compensation for the services of the Senators and Representatives, shall take effect, until an election of Representatives shall have intervened.

Unratified Amendments

During the past 200 years, there have been six proposed constitutional amendments submitted to the states that were not ratified. Those unratified amendments are listed below.

Subject of Amendment	Year Proposed
1. concerned the division of the seats in the House among the states	1789
2. revoked the citizenship of any American who accepted a title or honor from any foreign government	1810
3. prohibited any future amendment to the Constitution concerning slavery	1861
4. gave the federal government the power to regulate child labor	1924
5. Equal Rights Amendment; guaranteed women equal rights under the law	1972
6. gave the District of Columbia seats in Congress	1978

Congress' power to fix the salaries of its members is limited by delaying the pay increase until after the next congressional election. This gives voters an opportunity to react to that raise in pay.

The Road To Ratification: 1787–1789

1787

FEBRUARY 4
End of Shays' Rebellion

FEBRUARY 21
The Congress of the Confederation endorses plan to revise Articles of Confederation

MAY 25
Opening of Constitutional Convention in Philadelphia

MAY 29
Virginia Plan proposed

JULY 12
The Connecticut Compromise (I)

AUGUST 6
The committee drafts constitution document with twenty-three articles

AUGUST 6–SEPTEMBER 10
The Great Debate

AUGUST 16
The Convention grants Congress the right to regulate foreign trade and interstate commerce

SEPTEMBER 13–15
The Convention examines draft and makes a few changes

SEPTEMBER 17
All twelve state delegations vote approval of document

SEPTEMBER 20
Congress receives the proposed Constitution

SEPTEMBER 28
Congress submits the Constitution to special state ratifying conventions for ratification by nine states

1788

JANUARY 2
Georgia ratifies unanimously

JANUARY 9
Connecticut ratifies by vote of 128 to 40

FEBRUARY 6
The Massachusetts convention ratifies by close vote of 187 to 168

MARCH 16
Rhode Island holds popular referendum and voters reject the Constitution 2,708 to 237

JUNE 25
Virginia ratifies and the convention endorses a twenty-article bill of rights plus twenty other changes

JULY 2
Cyrus Griffin, President of Congress, announces the Constitution's ratification; committee appointed to prepare for change in government

JULY 26
New York ratifies by vote of 30 to 27 after Hamilton delays action

AUGUST 2
North Carolina declines to ratify until bill of rights is added

1789

JANUARY 7
Presidential electors chosen by ten of the ratifying states (all but New York)

FEBRUARY 4
Presidential electors vote; George Washington chosen as president, John Adams as vice-president

MARCH 4
The first Congress convenes in New York: 8 senators and 13 representatives in attendance, the remainder en route.

APRIL 1
The House of Representatives with 30 of its members present, elect Mublenberg as speaker

SEPTEMBER 2
Congress establishes Treasury Department

SEPTEMBER 22
Congress creates the office of Postmaster General

SEPTEMBER 24
Congress passes the Federal Judiciary Act, creating office of the Attorney General

SEPTEMBER 25
Congress submits to the states twelve amendments to the Constitution

JUNE 15
New Jersey Plan proposed

JUNE 19
The Convention decides to amend Articles of Confederation and devise new national government

JUNE 21
The Convention adopts two-year term for representatives

JUNE 26
The Convention adopts six-year term for senators

1787

AUGUST 25
The Convention prohibits Congress from banning foreign slave trade for 20 years

SEPTEMBER 6
The Convention adopts four-year term for the president

SEPTEMBER 8
Johnson, Hamilton, Madison, King, and Morris appointed to prepare final draft

SEPTEMBER 12
The draft, written primarily by Morris, is submitted to the Convention

OCTOBER 27
The first Federalist paper appears in New York City newspapers

DECEMBER 7
Delaware ratifies the Constitution, the first state to do so, by unanimous vote

DECEMBER 12
Pennsylvania ratifies the Constitution in face of opposition

DECEMBER 18
New Jersey ratifies unanimously

APRIL 28
Maryland ratifies by vote of 63 to 11

MAY 23
South Carolina ratifies by vote of 149 to 73

JUNE 21
New Hampshire becomes ninth state to ratify and the convention proposes twelve amendments

1788

SEPTEMBER 13
New York selected as site of the new government and date set for Congress' first meeting under the Constitution

SEPTEMBER 30
Pennsylvania is first state to choose its two senators—Morris and Maclay

OCTOBER 10
The Congress of the Confederation transacts its last official business

APRIL 6
The Senate, with 9 of 22 in attendance, chooses Langdon as temporary presiding officer

APRIL 30
Washington inaugurated in New York City as nation's first president under the Constitution

JULY 27
Congress establishes Department of Foreign Affairs (later changed to Department of State)

AUGUST 7
Congress establishes War Department

1789

NOVEMBER 20
New Jersey ratifies ten of the twelve amendments, the Bill of Rights, the first state to do so

NOVEMBER 21
North Carolina finally ratifies the original document by vote of 194 to 77

DECEMBER 19
Maryland ratifies Bill of Rights

DECEMBER 22
North Carolina ratifies Bill of Rights

Chapter 5 Review

1. **Answer these questions by reading the Preamble and Article I of the Constitution.**

   a. What part of the Constitution tells why the Constitution was written? _____

   b. For what branch of the government does this article outline its powers? _____

   c. What age must a person have reached to be eligible for election to the House of Representatives? _____

   d. What are two other requirements for a Representative? _____

   _____

   e. What is the length of a Representative's term of office? _____

   f. What age must a person have reached to be eligible for election to the Senate? _____

   g. What is the length of a Senator's term of office? _____

   h. How often must Congress meet? _____

2. **Answer these questions about Article II of the Constitution.**

   a. What is the length of a President's term of office? _____

   b. What age must a person have reached to be eligible for the office of President? _____

   c. What would prevent a person born in Germany from running for the office of President?

   _____

   _____

   d. What is the only kind of stated offense for which a President may not grant a pardon?

   _____

   e. What branch of the government approves many appointments made by the President?

   _____

3. **Answer these questions about Article III.**

   a. What is the name of the nation's highest court? _____

   b. How long shall justices of the Supreme Court hold their offices? _____

   c. How many witnesses must give testimony to the same act before a person can be convicted of treason? _____

4. **Answer these questions about the other articles of the Constitution.**

   a. Which article states that the Constitution is the supreme law of the land? _____

   b. Which article tells how many states had to ratify the Constitution before it could take effect? _____

   c. Which article sets forth the method of amending the Constitution? _____

   d. When does an amendment become a part of the Constitution? _____

   _____

   _____

Glossary

A

absolute monarch   all-powerful king and queen

affidavit   a written statement that the person making it swears to be true

affirmative action   a program aimed at ending the effects of past discrimination by giving favored treatment to minority groups

amend   to change or add to

B

bail   money given by accused persons to obtain their release while awaiting trial

boycott   to avoid using, buying, or dealing with as a means of protest

C

cabinet   presidential advisory board, composed of the heads of the executive departments

capital punishment   the death penalty

censure   to express disapproval

charters   legal documents issued by governments to define the purpose and privileges of corporations

citizenship   the status of a citizen, or member of a country, with all its duties, rights, and privileges

civil   relating to ordinary community life as opposed to criminal proceedings

civil rights   basic freedoms guaranteed to citizens by the Constitution

commission   a legal document that authorizes a person to perform official duties

common law   a system of law based on accepted customs, traditions, and past decisions

compromise   a settlement of differences in which each side gives up something

conciliator   one who settles disputes or restores friendship between

concurrent   happening at same time or shared

Continental Congress   elected representatives advising the colonists on policies regarding relations with Britain

cosmopolitan   having worldwide character or sophistication

D

delegate   one authorized to act as a representative for others

democracy   government by the people

direct democracy   a system of government in which people participate directly in decision making through voting on issues

discrimination   the act of judging people on the basis of prejudice

dissent   to disagree or withhold approval

due process   legal proceedings carried out according to established rules and principles

E

"Elastic Clause"   Constitutional power delegated to Congress, giving Congress the power to make laws needed to carry out its other responsibilities

envoy   a diplomatic representative of a government

establishment clause   part of the First Amendment to the Constitution prohibiting the government from setting up a national religion

executive   having the power to carry out laws

F

federalism   a system of government in which power is divided among national and state governments

federalize   to bring under the authority of the national government

free excuse clause   part of the First Amendment to the Constitution prohibiting the government from interfering in Americans' free exercise of their religious beliefs

fundamental rights   basic or essential freedoms

G

governor   person who carries out the laws enacted by a state legislature

grand jury   a group of people selected to hear evidence and decide whether a person should be charged with a crime

H-I

hamlet   a small village

impeach   to accuse or formally charge with misconduct

indentured servant   a person who agrees to work for another in return for travel expenses and maintenance

indictment   a formal charge usually brought by a grand jury

internment   confinement or imprisonment

J

"Jim Crow" laws laws passed by southern states in the nineteenth and twentieth centuries to force the segregation of the races

joint resolutions acts proposed by both houses of Congress and used to propose constitutional amendments

judicial having the power to tell what laws mean and decide if they are carried out fairly

judicial activism a philosophy that maintains that the Supreme Court should rule on constitutional questions and issues of public policy as often as possible

judicial restraint a philosophy that maintains that the Supreme Court should not make public policy and should take action only when the Constitution is clearly violated

judicial review the process by which the federal courts review congressional or presidential actions and declare them constitutional or unconstitutional

jurisdiction authority

K-L

legislative having the power to make laws

legislature section of the government responsible for making laws

libel intentional injury to a person's reputation

limited monarchy a government in which the rule of the king and queen is held in check by a constitution or by another part of the government

M-N

militias military forces that are on call for service in emergencies

nomination the process of selecting candidates to run for public office

O-P

override to rule against or declare invalid

Parliament British law-making body

plea bargain the process in which an accused person agrees to plead guilty to a less-serious crime

political party an organized group of people that seeks to control government through the winning of elections and the holding of public office

popular sovereignty self-government based on the will of the people

preamble an introductory statement

precedent a legal decision that serves as an example in later court cases

presumption of innocence the assumption that someone is innocent until proven guilty of a crime

probable cause valid reason for police to search or arrest

proportional representation a system of representation based on differences in population size between areas

prosecutor the government official who seeks to prove the guilt of an accused person

Q

quorum the minimum number of members who must be present for the valid transaction of business

quota a specified number or proportion used in affirmative action programs

R

radical fundamental or extreme

ratify to give formal approval

repeal officially withdraw

representation elected leadership

republic a system of government in which people elect representatives to govern them; also known as representative government

reverse discrimination treating a group of people unfairly in an attempt to help another group already suffering unfair treatment

revolutionary favoring a great change

S

salutary neglect policy of the British government during the colonial period, when the British allowed the American colonists to rule themselves as long as self-rule also benefitted Britain

segregate to separate people on the basis of race, class, or ethnic background

succeed to follow after and take over rank or title

successor a person who replaces or follows another

sue to seek justice through the legal process

T

tariff charges or taxes placed by the government on certain imported goods

tyranny a government in which a single ruler possesses complete power

U-Z

veto to reject or prevent a legislative bill from becoming law

writ of *habeus corpus* a court order requiring the government to release a prisoner unless good cause for imprisonment can be shown

writ of *mandamus* document that mandates, or requires, a public official to perform certain duties